This is the story of love and of faith; but even more it is a testimony to the grace and utter trustworthiness of God Himself. David Ellis interweaves personal story, filled with joy and grief and challenge, service in Asia and in the UK, with profound reflection on Scripture and the conviction that even in the darkest times God is still Lord of heaven and earth and history and thus to be trusted. This is not simplistic, sometimes the pain is raw, and David expresses that with deep honesty. But it is the journey of faith David and his beloved wife Adele walked as they fixed their eyes on Jesus. Here are the contours of true discipleship. Read and ponder!

Rose Dowsett
Retired member of OMF International, former Vice-Chair of WEA
Mission Commission, lecturer and author

Jesus frequently used parables in His teaching to help ordinary people connect spiritual truths with practical life circumstances. Likewise, David Ellis has shared powerful biblical truths through the prism of his life and ministry to help us readers see and feel the implications in our own circumstances. David's honesty and touches of humor in speaking of lessons learned enables us to better grasp God's unique work in each of our lives and to motivate us to press on and finish life well. Many biographies focus on what the person accomplished, but in reading David's story, I was captured more by spiritual truths that I need to embrace to bring glory to God and to fulfill His purpose for my life.

Dan Bacon
Leadership Consultant, OMF

This book does not tell us how to find God. Instead, it shows us how God finds us through Jesus Christ. David Ellis weaves together many rich, unwavering biblical principles with all the changing seasons of his personal life, demonstrating fear, pain, and suffering, yet faith, peace, and confidence. Ellis encourag   the frightening turmoil of the 'o   d today, taking heart in the prom   ) suffers, and who holds the futur   rist is our witness. Ellis' vulnerability and transparency stand out in this heart-warming and deeply moving book, and everyone should read it to the very end.

Patrick Fung
Director, OMF International

For those who, in life's uneven circumstances, trust in the Sovereignty of God, the book brings great reassurance. Behind life's unexplained challenges & difficulties, our loving Father works for our good. David's account of his eventful life, with his excellent exposition of God's Word adroitly applied, inspires us to run the race 'marked out for us' with fresh resolution and faith.

For those lost in the misty flats of shifting values and shaking foundations, this book brings hope. We are given solid biblical foundations pointing to Christ Himself on which we can build a secure life: 'Christ in you the hope of glory'.

The anxieties, warmth, humour, and trust in the Lord that come through, have not been put together to enhance the readability of the book. They are the authentic David, as he is and as I have known him many years.

David Pickard
Former OMF General Director

Rich treasures from two rich, rich lives. Sandwiched by their own love story at the beginning and the end, David Ellis writes beautifully and profoundly, and challenges us as readers to a faith that is daring and uncommon today.

Os Guinness
Author of *The Call: Finding and Fulfilling the Central Purpose of Your Life*

David quotes from Habakkuk, Job, the Gospels, and many other parts of Scripture, and links these with real life experiences in England, Indonesia, Singapore and Scotland. He quotes Lloyd-Jones, Keller, Mangalwadi and Kendrick and tells how truths that flow through them work themselves out in daily experience of illness, frustration, fear and doubt ... and how this all happens across the many cultures into which David and his family immersed themselves. Then in recounting his wife's illness and death David doesn't hesitate to bare his soul, and grasp the sovereign compassionate promises of God.

As you read, you'll walk with David and almost feel his pulse beat. You'll laugh. You'll ponder deeply your life's experiences as you measure yours against his. You'll be spurred on to greater trust in the Way, the Truth and the Life. Enjoy and grow.

Robert Benn
Minister of the Presbyterian Church of Australia

From airplane drama, rioting and political turmoil to the darkness of the Dunblane massacre and caring for his wife through 'the long goodbye' of Alzheimer's disease, David Ellis gives us a wonderful memoir of a grace-girded life.

Through all the Changing Scenes distils the lived-out wisdom and Biblical insights of a remarkable journey – from the assembly lines of Ford Cars to 22 years of Missionary work in Indonesia to church ministry in Scotland. David is a man who has experienced danger, sorrow and difficulties in some of their rawest forms. Yet what he has given us is a warmly written book, full of Scriptural reflection, that will both move and instruct its readers to see God's faithfulness in every part of life.

Andrew Hunter
Scotland & North of England Director, Fellowship of Independent
Evangelical Churches

Penned by a veteran missionary, *Through All the Changing Scenes* records the stories of God's faithfulness and mysterious providence in the pain, triumph, and silence of the mission field. This book is a must-read for those fresh in the early years of their missionary venture and for those struggling to finish strong through the grind of their missionary calling. This book is a testimony that God is faithful and He is sovereign. Read it and be reminded that God rules over the nations.

E.D. Burns
International missionary
Director of the MA in Global Leadership at Western Seminary

THROUGH

A Lifelong

ALL THE

Experience of God's

CHANGING

Unfailing Care

SCENES

DAVID W. ELLIS

CHRISTIAN
FOCUS

Copyright © David W. Ellis 2020

paperback ISBN 978-1-5271-0557-7
epub ISBN 978-1-5271-0632-1
mobi ISBN 978-1-5271-0633-8

10 9 8 7 6 5 4 3 2 1

Published in 2020
by
Christian Focus Publications Ltd,
Geanies House, Fearn, Ross-shire,
IV20 1TW, Great Britain.
www.christianfocus.com
Cover design by Pete Barnsley
Printed by Bell & Bain, Glasgow

CONTENTS

Foreword

It is a special personal privilege to have the opportunity to write the 'trailer' for *Through All the Changing Scenes of Life*.

The source of the title may be less well known today than it once was. The words, long familiar to many Christians, form the opening line of a hymn written three hundred years ago by Nahum Tate and Nicholas Brady. The themes that run through that great hymn have been the background music to David Ellis's life.

Anyone familiar with the hymn itself will probably assume this is a book for people going through rough times, encountering unexpected difficulties, facing trials, and needing encouragement. It is indeed that. But it is much more.

For one thing *Through all the Changing Scenes of Life* is an adventure story. It follows the life of a young engineer who finds himself taken from an automobile factory in England to the Far East, not only to a world that was different—in culture, language, food, and much else—but also dangerous. Few of us find ourselves in the middle of a revolution! And fewer people who do, when ordered by the British authorities to leave the country, have the conviction that they are under a higher authority and have a deeper loyalty to a greater kingdom!

So, there are pages in this book that read like a novel— one in which the facts are more exciting than the fiction because they took place in the real world.

In addition to danger, *Through all the Changing Scenes of Life* has the special ingredient Hollywood recognizes makes a good movie: *romance*. For here is the story of two people, very different in both temperament and gifts, who encounter one another and then come to realise that in each other they have found their destiny. And like all great romances, it is a story full of challenges, obstacles, sacrifices, and, yes, loss. It is the story of the faithfulness of God but also an account of a God-sustained and beautiful faithfulness to the promise 'to have and to hold from this day forward, for better, for worse, for richer, for poorer, in sickness and in health, to love and to cherish till death do us part'.

But there is still more. For this is also a book of instruction and devotion. Running through its pages are reflections on the Christian life which are full of the insight of Scripture and the wisdom of experience.

There is, indeed, something for everyone.

David Ellis and I were first in the same room almost fifty years ago at a Missions Conference at which we were both speaking. He was already a missionary of some years, while I was a very young minister. Thereafter I began to hear his name mentioned as a missionary with The Overseas Missionary Fellowship (now O.M.F. International). Years later he became one of my ministers; and so developed a friendship that eventually came full circle as we found ourselves members of the same congregation in St Peter's Free Church in Dundee.

I mention this because it helps to explain why, a couple of years ago, we were standing together boarding a plane in Dubai airport at about three o'clock in the morning body time. We were travelling together to a conference in Jakarta, Indonesia—the very country where David and Adèle Ellis had served for many years.

As the jet bridge filled up with Indonesians, I realized I was witnessing something remarkable. Just beside me (who was capable only of smiling to the Indonesians who surrounded us!) David had engaged in effortless conversation with some of them—in obviously fluent Indonesian!

It was as though he was now back in the world for which he had been made. It all seemed so natural. I was as fascinated as I was impressed! It felt like a scene in a movie where we discover our hero is in fact a brilliant linguist!

But then my eyes seemed to put on a wide-angle lens, and I found myself watching other Indonesians watching David and saw their evident amazement that he was speaking their language like one of themselves! I saw the kind of look on their faces that people must have seen in Jerusalem on the Day of Pentecost when visitors to Jerusalem were stunned to hear the apostles speak to them in their own tongue.

'He speaks Indonesian like an Indonesian' I was later told—by Indonesians! I saw then what I had long suspected. This man was much bigger than he seemed to those who knew him only in the West. If only the younger people in the church would sit down beside him and say 'Mr Ellis, tell me about yourself; what's your story? How did you get here?' they would be 'blown away'!

I later asked David, 'How did you do that, break into fluent Indonesian after twenty years away from Indonesia?'

His response? A simple 'I don't know'. I suppose the truth is that God had specially 'wired' him to serve in the Far East. But his answer was also indicative of the kind of man David Ellis is—more concerned to reflect Christ whose love and care he has received than that he should reflect on his own extraordinary gifts; more committed to using his gifts in serving others than to admire them in himself; more focused on Christ Himself than on anything he might accomplish for Christ.

These pages breathe that same spirit. That is why this is a story worth reading. I feel sure you will enjoy it. More than that I think it will help you to trust in, to love and to serve the same Lord who has guided David Ellis

> Through all the changing scenes of life,
> In trouble and in joy,

and it will, I hope, encourage you to say with him,

> The praises of my God shall still
> My heart and tongue employ.

Sinclair B. Ferguson

Author's Preface

In *Through all the Changing Scenes*, I have written from a biblical perspective, drawing on the practical down-to-earth life experience I have gained from more than fifty-seven years in Christian ministry, mostly between South East Asia and the UK.

My objectives were to write for Christian readers in an accessible way that is practical, rather than academic, so as:

a   To undergird the truth that the fear of God is the beginning of wisdom; and that when we learn to fear Him we have nothing else to fear and can hold on to the faithfulness of God, no matter how small and weak we may feel ourselves to be. God can be trusted.

b   To encourage a more biblical understanding of the sovereignty and providence of God in the frightening turmoil of the organised insanity of our world today.

c To distinguish between 'religion' and saving faith in union with Christ – touching the heart of the gospel.

d To encourage those who have put their faith and trust in God to understand that 'in trouble and in joy,' such as we experience 'in all the changing scenes of life' as we follow Christ, sickness or health, riches or poverty, are not works of chance but all come to us from His fatherly hand. And that all He sends to us 'in this vale of tears' will be used for the good of making us more like Christ. This as Almighty God He can do, and this, as our loving Father, He will do.

My prayer is that these pages may help those who accept the Lordship of Christ and seek to rest in His providential care as the central pivot around which the changing scenes of their life rotate, to have the confident assurance that He will not fail them. Indeed, He cannot fail for He is God and He has pledged His Word. And that is irrespective of whether we find ourselves in trouble or in joy.

In the words of a hymn based on Hebrews 13:5, 6:

> The soul that on Jesus hath leaned for repose,
> I will not, I will not desert to his foes;
> That soul, though all hell should endeavour to shake,
> I'll never, no never, no never forsake.[1]

The title *Through all the Changing Scenes* … comes from a paraphrase of Psalm 34 by Tate and Brady:

> Through all the changing scenes of life,
> In trouble and in joy,
> The praises of my God shall still
> My heart and tongue employ.

---

1. Anon, 'How firm a foundation, ye saints of the Lord', 1787.

Of His deliverance I will boast,
Till all that are distressed
From my example courage take
And soothe their griefs to rest.

O magnify the Lord with me,
With me exalt His name;
When in distress to Him I called,
He to my rescue came.

O make but trial of His love;
Experience will decide
How blest are they, and only they,
Who in His truth confide.

Fear Him, ye saints, and you will then
Have nothing else to fear;
Make you His service your delight;
Your wants shall be His care.[2]

David W. Ellis

---

2. Tate, Nahum, and Brady, Nicholas, 'Psalm 34', from *New Version of the Psalms of David* (1696).

CHAPTER 1

Trust and Obey

The Providence of God is like Hebrew words – it can be read only backwards. – John Flavel

Can I really trust God? For this?

I am sitting surrounded by some 28,500 tons of steel in a small third-class cabin. Steerage. Deep down in the hull of the S.S. Orcades. It is about to sail from Tilbury Docks for Singapore. The ship's deep-throated foghorn has just sounded a mighty blast and an announcement has come over the Tannoy along the lines of – 'Would all visitors not sailing with the ship please disembark – the ship is about to sail.' I am gripped with a sense of panic. On the dockside my parents and friends from my local church have come to see me off.

The panic is because I have not managed to say goodbye to Adèle. She was gone and now it was too late to see her to say goodbye before the ship would leave. I rushed around feverishly trying to find her, only to have to stand and scan the hundreds of faces on the quayside looking down from the ship's rail.

Through the gossamer of paper streamers reaching out from the ship as it edged slowly away, I finally managed to see what was, for me, the dearest face in all the world. We did our best to wave meaningfully to each other, but the sense of emptiness and desolation left an aching emptiness I feel to this day. We knew we would not see each other again for at least another twelve months. And, at that point of time, there was no guarantee we would ever come together. It was a matter of hope and trust.

'Is that your fiancée?'

A voice at my shoulder. It was one of the missionary candidates who had just joined our ship from the United States, seeing Adèle's lively response she had put two and two together and made five.

'She's not my fiancée …' I hesitated, 'We're going to get engaged as soon as she gets accepted.'

'I've heard that before – it doesn't always work!'

A child of missionaries in Latin America, maybe she had had some experience to make her think she was qualified to speak. What she never knew was just how near she came to being thrown over the side of the ship! Luckily for her, I was hurting so badly that I was too upset to say any more. Her words had reached where they had no right to trespass. We were trusting God. But were we just naive?

As the ship left ever so slowly, I found that moment desolating. Traumatic. The feeling of not being able to find Adèle and the memory of that day has never left me. I don't now expect that ever to change in this life. Perhaps it helps me not to judge others before I have learned to understand what might lie buried in the memories they carry. People need to be handled with kid gloves, always with care.

Leaving Adèle behind I didn't need reminding of the 'risk.' I was already fearful. Both of us by that stage were deeply in love, and our relationship had, from its very beginning, been a mutually agreed step of faith. Her comment was an attack on our commitment to put God first in our relationship. Had we got it wrong? Could we really trust God?

A few years earlier, 1959, and my first term at the Bible Training Institute in Central Glasgow, we were several weeks into the autumn term. Around 180 students all living in the hostel type rooms of what was affectionately called 'the Grim Old Castle of Bothwell Street', long since demolished to make way for faceless office buildings.

The student body, of men and women, had been drawn from all over the UK and Europe. We were all dedicated to learning how to study the Bible and were constantly challenged to focus on evangelism. The College Principal, Andrew MacBeath, had been a missionary in the Belgian Congo and South Africa. He had experienced a time of revival in Congo and kept the vision for missionary work on the foreign field constantly before us.

I had come direct from working in the drawing office as a young Production Engineer in a newly constructed factory assembly line at the Ford Motor Company in Dagenham. I had left Ford to study with a very strong determination that nothing was going to distract me from those biblical studies. After engineering, being more of an artisan than an academic, the reading of so many books and the writing of essays was a challenge. But the opportunity to get down to studying God's Word was thrilling.

One evening, after the end of the statutory evening study period when all of us were meant to be in our rooms until nine o'clock – (things were quite regimented in those days) – I took a jaunt downstairs to the basement kitchens for supper. As residential students, we were free to make up supper from the day's leftovers. Bubble and squeak – an unhealthy fried up mash of potatoes and vegetables, was a favourite! It was then I saw her! She was a new face, standing by the tall, old-fashioned aluminium milk churn filling a jug from a long-handled ladle, an older woman by her side. She wasn't a student. I hadn't seen her before.

Briefly our eyes met. She disappeared. There was just 'something' about her.

'Who's *that* girl?'

'Oh, that's Adèle – the Principal's daughter. She lives in the flat upstairs.'

I didn't get to see her for weeks after that brief encounter. She was studying French and Italian at Glasgow University from which she would graduate with a double first. She didn't appear at any of the college lectures. I put the 'distraction' out of my mind.

The MacBeath family lived in a small flat within the precincts of the college. The Principal, a godly man with a pastoral heart, always made himself as available to the students as was humanly possible. But it was not always easy to track him down in the labyrinthine passages of the Grim Old Castle. One place where we knew we could find him was when he retreated to his flat at lunchtime.

As students we ate first in the downstairs dining room. If we wanted to find the Principal, the temptation was to rush upstairs and ring the doorbell of his flat. For him the students always had priority and if one of us came to the door he would jump up from the table and shepherd us into his study just across the corridor. The family, however, didn't enjoy the disruptions! So, it seems Adèle was commissioned by her mother and three brothers to contact the Student's President and get him to flag up that the family would appreciate some uninterrupted peace at mealtimes.

It just 'happened' that I was the one she had to contact.

To cut a long story short, we met one afternoon over a coffee. Despite our different backgrounds we soon discovered we seemed to have a great deal in common – that sense of companionability there from the start. So, when I suggested we might meet again – she didn't say no!

As term progressed, I faced the crisis of trying to be sure as to God's will for our relationship. Each week I had gone to the China Inland Mission (CIM) prayer meeting at the home of Henry and Mary Guinness. There was a growing sense that God might want me to be a part of an answer to the prayers I was praying for the work of the Mission. With Mary's warm hospitality and tempting Chinese meals cooked for the students before the meeting, not a few of us were helped to look East in those days.

Now the college 'house rules' at BTI were that if you wanted to 'go out' with any 'member of the opposite ...,' then you had to check it out with the Principal to get his blessing. How old-fashioned that would seem today! But if falling in love with any student at BTI presented a challenge, courting the principal's daughter was of a different order of magnitude.

At one of the routine weekly de-briefing sessions with Mr MacBeath, when I was expected to report back on student matters, he was just about to bow his head to pray, which was his way of saying the session is over, when he looked straight up at me and said:

'Well, David, and is there anything else that you want to tell me?'

It was now or never. I'm not sure exactly what I said but he got the message – I wanted to be allowed to see more of his daughter!

For a moment he just sat and looked full at me. I'm sure he must have heard my heart beating. Then without a word he shot out of his chair and across the corridor to his flat. I sat waiting all alone staring at the pile of books on his desk. I don't know who he had gone to talk to or whether he had an inkling that I was going to ask his permission. Adèle wasn't around. To this day he never explained his abrupt departure but when he came back and sat down in his swivel chair, he simply bowed his head and started to pray – a pattern that was as natural to him as breathing. He hadn't said no! I took his prayer to be 'yes!'

My dilemma then was what to say to Adèle? We had become friends, often walking home from Church and chatting happily together, but I wanted our relationship to go up a gear. Should I send off my application papers to the Mission and then ask if she would be interested in the possibility of joining me? Not very romantic! Or should I delay applying to the Mission until after I knew how she felt? What would I do if she said she was not sure about pursuing our friendship on those terms?

Increasingly it had become clear to me that if I didn't apply to the CIM before going any further in our relationship, I would be disobeying a sense of what, I was now as sure as I could be, that God was asking me to do. It seemed to be the light he had given me for the next step. The challenge was to obey and take that step, to put obedience first and trust the Lord for whether our relationship was to progress or must end.

It could easily be argued that Jesus' words, 'Seek first his Kingdom and his righteousness and all these things will be given to you as well' (Matt. 6:33), could have been applied differently. But for me it had become painfully clear that the issue was one of obedience. I was convinced God was asking me to trust His promise that He would take care of whatever was to happen next.

I made the decision. I put the envelope with my completed application papers into the post office at Wellington Street. Then I invited her out for a cup of Chinese tea at the Sauchiehall Street Chinese restaurant – as a penniless student, a cup of tea was all I could afford! I had the distinct impression that the Chinese waiter was at a loss to know why we would want a cup of Chinese tea without first ordering a meal! I told her that I had just posted my application to the CIM and wondered if she would be interested in the possibility, one day, of joining me? She smiled. We downed our tea and walked out of the restaurant shyly holding hands. She hadn't said no!

Soon after Adèle graduated from University, she went off to study at Rome University. I was in Glasgow. She was writing up a doctoral thesis on the critics of a famous Italian author. I was studying theology. She returned to Glasgow from Rome. I was accepted for the candidate course by CIM down in London. I left for Singapore. She stayed home in Glasgow teaching Italian at extension classes under the aegis of Glasgow University. Meanwhile I was out in Singapore waiting for a visa to get to Indonesia.

As my companion at the ship's rail learned, we had agreed that we would only get engaged if the Mission finally accepted Adèle based on her missionary calling. It was another step along the road in trying, albeit with so many weaknesses and failings, to put what we understood to be the Lord's will, first for our life together. To our great joy she was accepted. In faith I had left an engagement ring for her with her father before I left. On Christmas Day 1962, she was in Glasgow and I was in Singapore, and father put the ring on her finger. Our truly long-distance engagement sealed with a ring! God had not disappointed the step of faith we had taken. Finally, she hadn't said no! She had said yes!

However, the saga of literally passing like ships in the night continued. I was studying Malay and living with a kind Muslim family in a traditional Malay Kampong in Singapore waiting for a visa. Almost exactly twelve months to the day the family joined me on the dockside with a bunch of orchids to welcome her as she disembarked from the S.S. Orsova. It was also the very day, of all things, my visa to leave for Indonesia came through. But we had a couple of glorious weeks together and once more we separated. I flew off to Jakarta courtesy of Pan Am. Any further 'courting' could only be done, as before, by long-distance letter writing.

I say 'long-distance' since Indonesia and Singapore/Malaysia were in a state of aggressive confrontation at the time. It certainly didn't make things easy. There were no direct communications. Of course, it was long before the days of computers and the Internet. No email. No phones. No word processors. The political conflict between Singapore and Java, fuelled by the Communist Party, meant any letter I sent to Singapore had to go via our Bangkok office and be forwarded to Adèle under a different cover. Not exactly confidential! Similarly, any reply to Java took, at the very least, another two weeks provided OMF Bangkok was on its toes.

Some months later Adèle finally arrived by ship to Jakarta. To avoid the problems of the hostilities, she had to come via Hong Kong. By then I was already living a long day's journey down country in Central Java. All in all, I think we must have spent more than three years apart in different geographical locations. And, just to add to our suspense, the Mission stipulation was that we were to wait a further twelve months in different locations after the end of her Orientation Centre language studies in Singapore before we could get married. I think we were just a few weeks short of the specified time, but a dispensation was applied for and our Field Director was a sympathetic and well acclimatised follower of Indonesian rubber time! Finally, a civil wedding was conducted by a Muslim government official in front of the British Consul. Two weeks later Soesilo, minister of the Javanese Church which was sponsoring us, arranged an exotic Javanese wedding for us in Salatiga. That was August 1964.

However, within five months of getting married, Adèle became ill. We were many miles from a doctor or any hospital. She developed pneumonia with the complication of a collapsed lung. When eventually we managed to get to a Christian hospital in Jogjakarta she was diagnosed with pulmonary tuberculosis and hospitalised.

With the rise of the Communist Party, said to have the largest membership outside of the Soviet Union in those days, the country was in economic meltdown and political turmoil. Inflation had gone through the roof – we never knew what our money would buy by the next day, let alone the next week. The hospital staff did what they could. But it was proving almost impossible to get hold of medications and her health deteriorated seriously. After a couple of distressing months in Bethesda Hospital, Jogjakarta, we managed to secure permission to get an exit visa to Singapore and eventually found a P & O ship to take us back to the UK. So many unanswered questions.

Was this now to be the end of our missionary work? What did the future hold? What was to become of our missionary calling? Had all those hours spent in language learning been just a waste of time? Those questions surfaced again. Had we got it wrong? Could we really trust God?

Through the kindness of friends back home in Scotland we managed to have a year of good medical care and rest in the cool clean air of Braemar in the Scottish Highlands. Then in the goodness of God, the hope He had given us when He called us was not disappointed. Adèle's health recovered and we were eventually allowed to go back to Indonesia in 1966 just in time to find the country reeling in the chaotically dangerous aftermath of the failed Communist coup. The coup and the bloodbath that followed on had taken place just months after we shipped out of Indonesia in 1965. As we returned the killings were still going on – politically it was a dangerous time – it was tricky to know how and where to put our feet – but the Lord proved to be what the Psalmist said He would be: 'Our refuge and strength, an ever-present help in trouble' (Psalm 46:1). We hadn't got it wrong. He was our refuge. He was our strength. He could be trusted. He was faithful.

Four boys, three born in Java, one in the UK. A year in the International Headquarters Singapore. Then back home to a ministry based in Scotland by 1983! Happily married for fifty-two years and now with ten grandchildren, we discovered through life that the Lord is always faithful to His promises. He has been good to us, summed up in the verses of a hymn that, in some ways has come to be the anthem of the CIM – OMF International.

How good is the God we adore,
Our faithful, unchangeable friend;
His love is as great as his pow'r
And knows neither measure nor end.

'tis Jesus the first and the last;
Whose Spirit will guide us safe home.
We'll praise him for all that is past,
And trust him for all that's to come.[1]

And if you wonder why this sketchy personal biopic should begin this book you will need to read further. Compared with all the early challenges at the beginning of our missionary life – bigger challenges lay ahead. We were yet to learn what it meant to take a step of faith and 'trust him for all that's to come' through all the changing scenes of life.

---

1. Hart, Joseph, 'How good is the God we adore' (1712-1768).

CHAPTER 2

From Fear to Faith

The remarkable thing about fearing God is that, when you fear God, you fear nothing else; whereas if you do not fear God, you fear everything else. – Oswald Chambers

It was late afternoon. Monsoon season in Borneo. The humidity was tangible. Winston, our lanky American pilot, was impatient. He kept one arm leaning on the door of the plane. Our missionary escort kept talking. Finally, one eye on the weather, his patience ran out.

'That's it – we take off right now!'

The small Helio Courier plane was to take us from Miri in East Malaysia flying north over Brunei to Lawas, The Borneo Evangelical Mission airstrip in Sarawak. The plane was unusual. Designed to take off and land on short runways. Ideal for the rough airstrips cut into the jungle. It had an amazing ability to almost hover as it came in to land at low speeds.

Two other passengers were already seated and waiting patiently for us to get in. I climbed into the front seat alongside the pilot and strapped on the harness. The single engine roared to life. We rattled down the runway. The yoke came back and in no time we were airborne.

Below us the jungle looked like a sea of broccoli laced with yellowish brown rivers. The altimeter soon indicated we had climbed past 3,000 feet as we headed upwards towards a magnificent vista of massive pillars of white-cotton wool clouds. It felt like floating in a blue space through the white columns of some celestial cathedral. To me it was unforgettably beautiful. Winston, however, did not share my enthusiasm. I was soon about to find out why!

Just how we found ourselves folded into those clouds I have forgotten. Not surprising in the light of what happened next. What I do remember was that Winston was clearly unhappy. The more he tried to find a way through and out of the clouds the more we were trapped. What's more the plane began to pitch and roll violently in all directions like a cork bobbing in the sea. We felt very small. The plane felt flimsy. Vulnerable.

Winston battled at the controls. Solid chunks of rain battered noisily on the windscreen. The water obscured any visibility. All those beautiful blue spaces had vanished. Through the cascading curtain of water on the screen it was a complete whiteout. Looking down below the instruments I studied the little safety notice pinned to the dashboard by the manufacturer:

'No acrobatic spins or turns in this aircraft.'

I wondered what kind of safety margin the engineers had factored into their calculations when they drew up their design.

Suddenly Winston took us into a dive from 4,000 feet.

'I'm going to try and get under the weather,' he explained.

It didn't take much to understand why he would want to do that. But as we plunged, the wee plane shuddered and vibrated, and it was only as we began to emerge beneath the cloud the turbulence eased.

Relief, however, was short-lived. There, right ahead of us, loomed the very solid mass of what looked like the side of a mountain. Winston (with what I presume was his former military flying instinct) threw the plane dramatically sideways into a steep climbing turn and I wondered whether that would have been defined as an 'acrobatic spin or turn!' Gratefully we didn't hit anything and the plane, that felt more fragile than ever, held together as he levelled out! Our two Malaysian passengers made no attempt to suppress their fears or hide their emotions and my pulse rate was well above the normal to say the least.

I was scared! But what happened next did little for my pulse rate when I heard him mutter under his breath:

'Wow! I didn't expect that. Where are we?'

We were off course. Winston spread a map on his knees and peered through the streaming water on the windshield. The plane was flying better – for which I was truly thankful – but it was hard to pinpoint just where we were. The storm had blown us way off course towards rocky hillside.

At that point Winston flipped a switch to the side of a large circular dial; made various adjustments till a red light appeared accompanied by a regular series of beeping signals.

'There's a radio beacon that's broadcast from Brunei International Airport and I've locked onto it. We'll just follow the RDF.'

He was relieved. I was relieved. We were not totally cut off from the outside world!

You must remember we are talking of the days long before invention of the GPS systems we have in our cars which we now take for granted. The fact that the plane's RDF (Radio Direction Finder) had locked onto a radio beam being broadcast from the airport's control tower and by following that signal we were able to steer northwards to clear skies over the sea, seemed nothing short of miraculous to me at that time. As we emerged from the storm and out over the South China sea there was a wonderful sense of relief and Winston cheered visibly. A quick check on his map and he plotted a new course back towards the coast of Sarawak and on to Lawas.

It was not long before the longed-for strip of mown grass appeared ahead of us. Winston nosed the plane over the end of the runway and parked the Helio right in front of his wooden house as if nothing had happened. His wife ran out to meet us. He must have sensed I was bursting to tell her about our adventure and before he opened the door, he turned to me and simply said, 'Don't say a word!'

I understood. His wife had more than enough reasons to be anxious for him. Missionary Aviation jungle flyers live a dangerous life. We had been driven off course by the storm, lost and overwhelmed by forces over which we had no control. Some days later he flew me up-country where I was to speak at an Easter conference at a village called Ranau. The views of nearby Mount Kinabalu were spectacular and Winston gave me a lecture on how he could gain height by making use of the updraft from the 'thermals' which rose from the sides of the mountain. Out of the blue he said, 'Remember that dodgy flight from Miri?' As if I could forget!

'It was the thermal updrafts and downdrafts in those clouds that shook us. No joke – the plane could have broken up. We left it too late in the afternoon to leave with the Monsoon. Never again!'

So, I was not the only one who was afraid that day. But it was his knowledge of flying, his years of training, practical experience and access to a resource outside the storm he encountered that enabled him to handle his fear and keep control when at the mercy of forces that were beyond his control.

Most of us will have times facing storms not of our making. Circumstances beyond our control. Increasingly this is a fact of life for us as Christians. Increasingly pushed out to the margins by a secularised, humanist society in the West; facing aggression and open hostility in other parts of the world; the spectre of Global Terror; it is all too easy for us to become fearful.

Yet we have God's promise:

When you pass through the waters, I will be with you; and when you pass through the rivers, they will not sweep over you. When you walk through the fire, you will not be burned; the flames will not set you ablaze (Isa. 43:2).

And again, the promise He made to the pilgrims as they lifted their eyes to the rugged, bandit-infested hills which had to be walked through in order to reach their destination at Jerusalem:

He will not let your foot slip—
he who watches over you will not slumber;
indeed, he who watches over Israel
will neither slumber nor sleep.
The Lord watches over you—
the Lord is your shade at your right hand;
the sun will not harm you by day,
nor the moon by night.
The Lord will keep you from all harm—
he will watch over your life;
the Lord will watch over your coming and going
both now and forevermore (Ps. 121:3-8).

Facing life's storms, the forces in the world around us over which we have no control, the Word of God is a resource outside the storm. A resource to help us keep a cool head and a calm spirit; handle our fear and avoid going to pieces; an assurance that no situation we have to pass through is outside His control.

It is in our knowledge of God's Word, our years of learning to understand its truths, our walk with the Lord, our coming to know Him, to love Him, to trust and obey Him, that we discover the key to that resource beyond the storm. Fear and faith oppose one another. And for faith to overcome fear we need to know more of the one in whom our faith is placed.

The fear and fretting anxiety that come from danger or the threat of the unknown are negative. But there is an opposing fear that is positive, the fear born of faith. What the Bible defines as 'the fear of the Lord' does not mean being frightened, but rather having respect and a sense of awe and reverence that moves us to want to live our lives as an open book before Him. It means that we take what He says in His Word seriously and see doing His will as the most important thing in our lives. It means trusting Him for all He allows as He works all things together to make us more like Jesus, for 'we know that in all things God works for the good of those who love him, who have been called according to his purpose. For those God foreknew he also predestined to be conformed to the image of his Son …' (Rom. 8:28, 29).

That is why Paul could proclaim: 'If God is for us, who can be against us?' (Rom. 8:31). That is why the book of wisdom, Proverbs, begins by telling us that, 'the fear of the Lord is the beginning of knowledge' (Prov. 1:7). And later declares: 'He who fears the Lord has a secure fortress, and for his children it will be a refuge' (Prov. 14:26). Ecclesiastes, the philosophical treatise on the empty meaninglessness of living a life without God, ends up with the very same advice: 'Here is the conclusion of the matter: Fear God and keep his commandments, for this is the whole duty of man' (Eccles. 12:13).

That is the fear that drives out lesser fears – the fear of God – the sense of awe and reverence that Jesus needed His disciples to learn to have towards Him when He told them to get into the boat and ferry Him across the Sea of Galilee. He wanted them to learn that true fear of the Lord. He needed them to grasp who He really was. He knew it was going to take a storm in their lives for them to learn the truth about Him!

It had been a good day according to Mark 4:35-41. The crowd at the lakeside were so eager to hear Jesus preach that He had been forced to push off into the lake to get space. He made the boat into His pulpit and spent the day preaching. His disciples basked in the reflected glory of being associated with such a popular teacher. It was a very good day indeed.

In the evening, and tired out, Jesus told them to cross the lake to the other side and they took Him just as if He were any other passenger in their boat under their care and protection. He then went to sleep on a cushion in the stern. That was not a problem. The disciples were experienced sailors. They knew the lake. They had crossed it hundreds of times. It was their world. They knew what they were doing. Though you do wonder if Peter, the experienced fisherman who knew Galilee, might have seen the clouds gathering and had an inkling that a storm could be brewing.

All was fine – at least, until when the clouds did burst, and the wind howled and the storm became so bad that the waves broke right over into the boat. When Matthew tells us the story, he uses the Greek word for an earthquake[1]

---

1. Matthew. 8:24 Greek: 'σεισμος' – an earthquake.

to describe the storm as being 'furious.' This was no ordinary squall. It had such ferocity that these men found themselves at the mercy of elemental forces beyond their ability to control. They were gripped with fear. No wonder.

Earthquakes are terrifying. Once at a conference in a mountain resort in West Java we were woken in the middle of the night by a sound of rumbling such as we had never ever heard before. The bed was shaking violently. Adèle and I sat bolt upright. The door burst open. We could see the woven bamboo ceiling shaking. The light in the middle of the room bobbed up and down like a yo-yo. Both of us leapt out of bed and ran for the courtyard.

All round the quadrangle doors were opening. Under the clear tropical night, a motley group of us stood sheepishly in our night attire. Totally disoriented. There in the heart of the volcanoes and mountains of West Java we felt very small and vulnerable. There was nothing we could do. There are no switches to turn off an earthquake. Everything is out of control. At the sleepy hour of three o'clock in the morning it is hard to think. At the mercy of elemental forces, you are very aware of your mortality. That same knot of fear takes over. You are no longer in control. The feeling of helplessness is overpowering.

For the disciples, after such a good day with Jesus the suddenness and nature of the storm were totally unexpected. Their 'earthquake' had a life of its own and seemed about to end theirs. They were at its mercy. In panic they wake Jesus: 'Don't you care if we drown?' they cried above the noise.

Their question, literally, was: 'Don't you care if we perish?' They were convinced that they were about to die. Given the circumstances, they had a point.

It was Jesus who had told them to take Him across the lake. And it was because they had done exactly what He had asked of them that they found themselves in trouble. Clearly, for them obedience to Jesus was no guarantee of a charmed life without storms. Jesus never promises that for any who follow Him. A lesson we need to grasp when storms hit us. Jesus, in fact, spoke more of trouble (John 16:33) and persecution if we choose to take up the cross and follow Him. Many faithful followers of Jesus know a great deal about what that means for them. As we follow Him in this fallen world, He gives us no guarantees of health, wealth and prosperity. No offer of freedom from the ills common to mankind. No insurance against the realities of life. Just so here on the lake, it was precisely because the disciples had obeyed Him that they found themselves in desperate straits. It was no guarantee of an easy passage to the other side of the Sea. They no longer had control.

What happened next was scary. Jesus stood up and took control of the wind and waves. The implications of that proved even more frightening for them. The one who was so fully human that He could get worn out and sleep through an earthquake of a storm suddenly revealed Himself to His disciples to be the sovereign Creator – able to command the very elements in the world He had created. That really was way off the Richter Scale, terrifying!

Jesus could have ensured that the crossing went smoothly without any storms. But they would have missed out on that revelation of who He was. They would also have failed to learn a vital truth: dictating to God is not faith. 'How is it, that you have no faith?' He queried. Faith is not the power to manipulate God to get Him to do what we want Him to do. Faith is a trust in what God will do that He knows will ultimately be for our good and His glory.

It was because they believed in His powers that they were calling on Him. That is understandable but in Matthew's account they appear to be even more demanding –

telling Him what He ought to do. It was not, however, the confidence of faith that drove them to wake Him, but fear. Faith and fear are mutually incompatible, and they needed to learn.

Jesus asked them why they were fearful[2] – using a word that can mean 'timid' or even 'cowardly.' It was only when the truth as to who He was dawned on them that a paradigm shift took place in their thinking – their fear overtaken by terror. Literally Mark tells us: 'they feared a great fear.'[3] A fear that drove them to exclaim: 'Who then is this?' echoing the rhetorical question of the Old Testament writers speaking of God as the Creator: 'Who has gathered up the wind in the hollow of his hands? Who has wrapped up the waters in his cloak … what is his name and the name of his son?'[4]

No wonder a sense of awe overwhelmed them. They would have been very foolish not to be afraid. The Sovereign Lord who created the heavens and the earth and could control the elements was standing right there with them. In the light of that, everything paled into insignificance. And within that greater fear of the Lord they had nothing else to fear.

Mark links the story with the day's preaching when he says that Jesus did not say anything to them without using a parable (see Mark 4:34). This experience was one parable they would never forget. It must have helped to prepare them for that day when another earthquake would strike, and their world would be changed forever.

Jesus' popularity was about to wane. The watershed in His ministry comes as Peter makes his famous confession.

2. Mark 4:40; Greek: δειλοι – cowardly, timid, fearful.

3. Mark 4:41; Greek: εφοβηθησαν φοβον μεγαν – they feared a great fear.

4. Proverbs 30:4; Psalm 65:7 Psalm 107: 25-30 cf. Job 38:4-11; Isaiah 40:12; Job 26:8;38:8-9.

Jesus had asked – 'Who do people say the Son of Man is?' Peter has seen who He is. 'You are the Christ, the son of the living God' (Matt. 16:13-16). It was the high point. But from then on it seemed to be downhill all the way to the 'earthquake' of the cross.

So, Jesus warns that He must go to Jerusalem and suffer. More than that, He says 'he must be killed and on the third day be raised to life' (Matt. 16:21). This is too much for Peter. He takes Jesus aside and tries to set Him straight. But the path to the cross had been mapped out before the dawn of time. At this point of time, however, the disciples had no notion of what was in store for all of them.

Naively, they had their own ideas of what Jesus meant when He spoke of establishing His kingdom. Even after His resurrection their ideas about the kingdom of God were still earthbound as they asked Him: 'Lord, are you at this time going to restore the kingdom to Israel?' (Acts 1:6). God's plan and purpose of redemption for the nations had not yet dawned on them. The cross was a great earthquake – unwanted, unexpected, subjecting them to forces over which they had no power.

The cross may have been the first earthquake. But there were to be aftershocks. The religious and political powers that conspired to put Jesus to death now turned their spotlight on His disciples. Peter and John suddenly found themselves in trouble after healing a lame man and causing a general disturbance. They might well have felt like crying again: 'Lord, don't you care if we perish?'

However, before the Sanhedrin struck, they had experienced a different kind of 'earthquake' – Pentecost. The coming of the Holy Spirit had brought their understanding about Jesus into focus. The pages of Scripture came to life and the seemingly random jigsaw of events formed a picture. It was all there in the second Psalm which we will need to think more carefully about at some point. What the disciples were experiencing had been foretold. That realisation was to bring boldness. Peter was so convinced of these truths that he made his controversial claim when he said: 'Salvation is found in no one else, for there is no other name under heaven, given to men by which we must be saved' (Acts 4:12).

The Sanhedrin, surprised by this display of bold courage, 'realised that they were unschooled, ordinary men, they were astonished and took note that these men had been with Jesus' (Acts 4:13). What they had not grasped was that Jesus was still with them, as He had promised to be (See Matt. 28:20). Peter and John knew He was with them. So however fearful they might have been, they remembered with awe the one who commanded the wind and the waves. They could hold on to His faithfulness. He was with them whatever was going to happen to them. In such confidence, they knew there was nothing to fear but fear.

On another occasion, Jesus took His disciples aside and gave them this word about faith. He said: 'If you have faith as small as a mustard seed, you can say to this mountain, 'move from here to there,' and it will move. Nothing will be impossible for you' (Matt. 17:20). The mustard seed is tiny. But it is in its DNA to grow up quickly to become a large spreading tree. So, the point is that it is the one who is the object of our faith and what He wants to do in our lives, not the strength of our faith, that guarantees that He will perfect that work for our good and His glory.

Of course, we must be careful not to misapply what Jesus was saying. He was not giving us a carte blanche to expect God to supply all our longings for health, wealth and happiness. We are to frame our expectations in line with what the Bible teaches us. It is to misapply His words if we try to make it a key to getting what we think we want and what we think He ought to do for us. The lesson Jesus was reinforcing was to focus on the mighty one in whom our trust is placed, not our feelings.

A lesson underlined for me by a tale of two bridges. I was working in the Javanese Church. The minister, Domine Soesilo, was a tireless evangelist. In my early years in Central Java, I frequently went with him on his trips across the rice fields to the many small villages surrounding Salatiga. On one occasion he invited me to join a work party on an assignment to help build a small meeting-place for a newly formed group of believers. In order to reach the village, we had to cross a river. The bridge was a flimsy cat's cradle, made, I think, out of rattan and bamboo. The river, though small, seemed quite a way below. I was decidedly uneasy about trusting my weight to the crossing.

Soesilo, with his lightly built frame, swung his way across walking happily in rhythm with the swaying bridge. Being so much larger, and probably nearly twice his body weight, I hesitated. My obvious fear was, 'Would the bridge hold up?' Soesilo, amused at my hesitation, called back.

'No worries. Don't fear, Pak Ellis. It's strong enough!'

Fearful, I didn't share his confidence. My fear was greater than my faith at that point. However, tentatively, I stepped forward. In the event, I needn't have worried. The bridge was more than strong enough. I arrived safely in one piece to join the work party.

Some years later I had a very different experience. I was in Sulawesi travelling northwards along the unmade road that runs north from the Buginese village of Parepare to Makale in Toraja. It had been raining hard and our driver stopped when we came to cross a bridge at the bottom of a valley. The river was in full flood and our driver took stock.

The bridge certainly looked strong. It was built from large rocks. But he was weighing up the odds. He knew his bus was overloaded.

Politely we were told to get out and walk. We filed across the bridge and climbed a way up the steep valley road on the other side. I wondered why the driver needed to get us to walk on ahead. Whatever, the rain was refreshing, and it was a relief to stretch our legs on that ten-hour journey over the bumpy track. I had no sense of any fear.

The driver decided to drive across as quickly as he could and get it over with. The sound of its engine was drowned out by the noise of the water rushing against the bridge. We watched safely from the hillside as the bus drove up to collect us. We were just getting ready to get back on the bus and clamber our way to a seat through all the various goats, chickens and sacks stacked between the seats when someone shouted:

'Aduh! Jembatan! Habis! Hancur!'[5]

The bridge had disappeared with a roar in a tumbling pile of rocks rumbling away down the valley. The vibrations from the bus along with the force of the water had proved too much for it. I hadn't experienced the slightest fear when crossing. To me it looked well-built, unlikely to give way. Had I known what I was to witness as it collapsed I would not have been so confident! By contrast, no matter how timid my faith had been swaying across the river on the old rattan bridge, it was the strength of that bridge, not the strength of my feelings that took me safely to the other side.

The driver's judgment doubtless based on experience had been sound. We were all OK and the parable of those two bridges stays with me. It is not the strength of my faith

---

5. Indonesian: 'Wow! Bridge! Gone! Destroyed!'

or feelings that saves me but the strength of the one in whom my faith is placed! The more I get to know Him, the stronger my faith – the stronger I am able to face my fears.

With the experience of surviving many wild storms at sea, the old sailor, John Newton wrote:

'His love, in time past, forbids me to think He'll leave me at last in trouble to sink …'[6]

The disciples moved from fear to faith when they discovered that the one to whom they had called out in their fear was the Creator God who ruled the wind and the waves. No wonder they said, 'Who is this? Even the wind and the waves obey him!' (Mark 4:41). And no wonder they 'feared a great fear' – He was right there with them in their boat!

> Be still, my soul; the Lord is on your side;
> Bear patiently the cross of grief or pain;
> Leave to your God to order and provide;
> In every change he faithful will remain.
> Be still, my soul; your best, your heavenly Friend
> Through thorny ways leads to a joyful end.
> Be still, my soul; your God will undertake
> To guide the future as he has the past.
> Your hope, your confidence let nothing shake;
> All now mysterious shall be bright at last.
>
> Be still, my soul; the waves and wind still know
> His voice who ruled them while he dwelt below.[7]

6. Newton, John, 'Be gone unbelief' (1725-1807).

7. von Schlegel, Catharina, 'Be still my soul' (1697-1768).

CHAPTER 3

A Word to the Fearful

Man is born to trouble as surely as sparks fly upward. –
Eliphaz (Job 5:7)

Job was having a tough time. His world had collapsed. His nearest and dearest had died. He had lost all his possessions. He was desperately ill with what must certainly have seemed to him to be a life-threatening illness. He pours out his soul in an agony: 'What I feared has come upon me; what I dreaded has happened to me. I have no peace, no quietness; I have no rest, but only turmoil' (Job 3:25-6).

His first friend, Eliphaz, steps up and makes a rather fatuous statement: 'Man is born to trouble as surely as sparks fly upward.'

A colourful way of saying: 'Itu takdir Allah yang tidak bisa dirubah.'[1] Tough luck, Job. Life sucks! God's probably angry with you for your sins. Get used to it. Nothing you can do. As if that made Job feel any better! No wonder Job lashed out at Eliphaz and his friends: 'Miserable comforters are you all!' (Job 16:2).

It is only at the end of Job's story as God reveals Himself that Job says of the Lord: 'I know that you can do all things

---

1. Indonesian: 'It's the will of Allah that cannot be changed!'

… My ears had heard of you but now my eyes have seen you. Therefore I despise myself and repent in dust and ashes' (Job 42:2, 5-6).

And Eliphaz gets told off when God says to him: 'I am angry with you and your two friends, because you have not spoken the truth about me, as my servant Job has' (Job 42:7).

So what is the truth about God and His ways that finally brought Job to repentance? What brought him the comfort and healing he so needed when he faced his troubles? What reproved the so-called wise men when they thought they knew how to offer comfort?

We long for comfort. It's very human. We are living in uncomfortable days. Great nations rattle their swords. Ideological warfare, hatred and terror create fear on a global scale. There is much to make us fearful with all the uncertainties. Few, if any of us, can boast to escape those sentiments Job expressed, especially when personal tragedies hit us below the belt. There are also times for most of us when we could echo Job's words, if we are being honest:

'What I feared has come upon me; what I dreaded has happened to me. I have no peace, no quietness; I have no rest, but only turmoil.'

And just to be told to brush it all off as 'kismet' brings no comfort.

Adèle and I married and had our family of four boys in Java where we lived through the threatening tensions of Soekarno's revolution and all the political turmoil and Communist threat of the early sixties, then on into the eighties, before returning to Scotland. As missionaries in South East Asia and ministry back home in the UK, over a span of more than fifty-five years, life has had its fair share of 'sparks'. Some of those 'sparks' were painful at the time. Some of them are still painful. But how often we found it took those very 'sparks' to drive us to the Lord and strengthen our faith as we discovered:

> There is a hope that lifts my weary head,
> A consolation strong against despair,
> That when the world has plunged me in its deepest pit,
> I find the Saviour there![2]

As we find Christ is there in the deepest pits of life, we begin to find strength to face down our anxious fears.

We must avoid joining company with Job's 'miserable comforters,' but let the inevitable 'sparks' from the fires of life drive us back to God and His Word. There we will discover and rediscover that, when we have 'no rest but only turmoil,' peace comes as we rely on God's promises. We need to learn to hold on to the faithfulness of God if we want to find that 'the God and Father of our Lord Jesus Christ, the Father of compassion and the God of all comfort, who comforts us in all our troubles …,' (2 Cor. 1:3-4) proves to be our truest Comforter.

It is vital to grasp that, as a believer, you are 'in Christ.' And that reality has tremendous significance! Those two words 'in Christ' are the way New Testament believers liked to describe themselves. They didn't call themselves 'Christians' – that was a name the outside world used to describe them. It was not always meant kindly. NT believers saw themselves as living in union with Christ – being 'in Christ' and at the same time realising that the Spirit of Christ was living in them. So, with Paul they could say that it was not religion which saved them but Christ. While the outside world came to characterise their faith as being a 'religion' called

---

2. Stuart Townend & Mark Edwards Copyright © 2007 Thankyou Music (Adm. by CapitolCMGPublishing.com excl. UK & Europe, adm. by Integrity Music, part of the David C Cook family, songs@integritymusic.com).

'Christianity,' for them it was not a religion *about* Christ but a relationship *with* Christ. As Paul expressed it:

> 'For through the law I died to the law so that I might live for God. I have been crucified with Christ and I no longer live, but Christ lives in me. The life I now live in the body, I live by faith in the Son of God, who loved me and gave himself for me. I do not set aside the grace of God, for if righteousness could be gained through the law, Christ died for nothing!' (Gal. 2:20)

That is the very heart of the gospel in a nutshell. Paul had not found acceptance with God by trying to pull himself up by his religious bootstraps. He knew he was not saved by religion but could say the life he lived was no longer out of his own resources but by faith in the Son of God who lived in him by the Holy Spirit. No wonder he calls the gospel, 'the glorious riches of this mystery, which is Christ in you, the hope of glory' (Col. 1:27). And it was with that empowerment of the indwelling Spirit of Christ that he could say, 'I can do all things through Christ who strengthens me' (Phil. 4:13).

It is being united with Christ that defines us if we have put our faith and trust in Him as our Saviour and Lord. That has become our identity. Our story is now His story. Our sin became His. It was taken away from us on the cross. His righteousness became ours. It is now our story. His victory is ours; that is why we can trust Him with our lives just as Jesus trusted His father and could say, 'The reason my father loves me is that I lay down my life – only to take it up again' (John 10:17).

If we are believers then we are 'in Christ' and Christ is 'in us' by His Holy Spirit, no matter how we feel, no matter what we do, no matter where we go, no matter what we must face. It is not what we do, no matter how zealously religious we are, but it is what God does for us in Christ. The gospel, the good news, is the fact of 'Christ in you, the hope of glory.' And it is there in His mighty strength, not our feeble efforts at being religious, we have acceptance with God and find strength to face all the 'sparks' that life can throw up at us.

There is neither ground for despair nor room for pride. We must guard against the mind-set of the infamous flea that was in living in the ear of an elephant. We are back to bridges and parables again. When the pair of them crossed a rickety bridge, the elephant was treading so heavily that the bridge creaked and groaned. Once across the flea whispered in the elephant's ear, 'My, didn't *we* make that bridge shake!' As if! And when, by God's grace and by His power, we come through some trial, we must never give in to the temptation to think or boast as if by our own strength or gifts we had made it through.

Back in the nineteenth century in China, Dr James Hudson Taylor, founder of the China Inland Mission (now renamed OMF International), was under incredible pressure. He was facing the challenge, anxiety and responsibility for the direction and care of his missionaries, many living in remote primitive areas of Inland China. The burden of care and the need for assurance as he looked to God for all the financial needs of the Mission weighed heavily on his heart. He was fearful. However, he was driven back to the Word of God.

> When reading Mark 11:22 in Greek, he was struck with the words, Ἔχετε πίστιν θεου.' They seemed strangely new to him.
>
> 'Have (or hold) the faithfulness of God': surely it was a passage he had never seen before? Turning to the corresponding words in English he read (Mark 11:22): 'Have faith in God.' Ah, that was familiar enough; and something

within him whispered, 'the old difficulty!' How gladly would he have, and increase in, faith in God, if only he knew how! But this seemed entirely different. It laid the emphasis on another side of the matter in a way he found surprisingly helpful.

It was not 'have' in your own heart and mind, however you can get it, 'faith in God' but simply 'hold fast, count upon, His faithfulness' ... at all times and under all circumstances we are (to be) fully persuaded of this blessed truth. Not my faith but God's faithfulness ... The man who holds God's faithfulness will not be foolhardy or reckless, but he will be ready for every emergency. The man who holds God's faithfulness will dare to obey Him ... Abraham held God's faithfulness and offered up Isaac, 'accounting that God was able to raise him up, even from the dead ...' (Heb. 11:19 KJV).

Want of trust is at the root of almost all our sins and all our weaknesses; and how shall we escape it but by looking to Him and observing His faithfulness? ... How many estimate difficulties in the light of their own resources, and thus attempt little and often fail in the little they attempt!

All God's giants have been weak men, who did great things for God because they reckoned on His being with them ... Oh! beloved friends, if there is a living God, faithful and true, let us hold His faithfulness ...[3]

So, to 'have faith in God' is to count on the fact that He is faithful and to hold fast to the fact that He can be trusted. As our loving father and as Almighty God, He has both the power and the purpose to work with us as we encounter the inevitable 'sparks' that fly upward in this fallen world. He

---

3. From Howard Taylor, George, and Howard Taylor, Geraldine, *Hudson Taylor's Spiritual Secret* (Chicago, IL: Moody Press, 2009).

works them all together for the good purpose of making us more like His son, Jesus (see Rom. 8:28-29).

You are called to know Him, to love Him and to trust and obey Him. To know, to love, to trust and obey is the very essence of what it means to respect and reverence Him with a godly fear. It is as we learn to fear God we discover that we can count on His faithfulness and understand what Paul meant when he said: 'And the peace of God, which transcends all understanding, will guard your hearts and your minds in Christ Jesus' (Phil. 4:7).

It is that fear of God in a truly biblical sense that will help us discover, come what may, we have nothing else to fear.

A verse from the old paraphrase of Psalm 34 by Tate and Brady puts it neatly:

> Fear Him, ye saints, and you will then
> Have nothing else to fear:
> Make you his service your delight,
> Your wants shall be his care.[4]

---

4. Tate, Nahum, and Brady, Nicholas, 'Psalm 34', from *New Version of the Psalms of David* (1696).

CHAPTER 4

A Perspective from Global Terror

… Disillusioned, and not a moment too soon. – C.S. Lewis

I watched the bubbles. Normally bubbles rise. These were falling. Closer and closer they travelled down the tube. I thought there weren't supposed to be any bubbles in an intravenous drip. Guiltily they scurried out of sight through the intravenous cannula in the back of my hand. They were inside – somewhere.

Questions, stimulated by fever, tumbled around my mind. Aren't you supposed to make sure there aren't any bubbles? Did the nurse not see them when she changed the drip? How many bubbles could you get into your veins before a clot formed? The man in the bed next to me has a deep vein thrombosis. Did he get too much air into his veins?

I had driven myself to hospital after battling to preach through the pain barrier at a church in London. By the time I arrived at the hospital, the pain had become intense. Several years of dysentery in Java had done little to help my digestive system. Now a major intestinal infection was threatening the need for surgery. I was in considerable discomfort as I lay in the hospital ward – the 'why' and the 'what if' questions never far from my mind. It was hard not to be fearful.

Suddenly an animated nurse burst into the ward.

'Switch on the TV! Something's happening in New York!'

It was September 11th, 2001. All eyes in the ward focused on the screen. Who could forget where they were when those first images ploughed into our minds? Tied by an intravenous drip to a hospital bed, I was a captive audience. The bubbles forgotten. My 'whys' and 'what-ifs' faded into insignificance. This was big. The world had changed. As the horror of it all began to sink in, any fears I had felt for myself moved to a different plane. Where was God when all this was happening?

'The Day that Changed the Modern World' was how one newspaper headline summed it all up. But the world did not change. We did. Our perspective changed. Our eyes opened to reality. The world had declared its colours.

Ever since Adam chose to ignore his Maker's directions, evil has been present in our world. Like the cancer it is, evil does not discriminate. Its nature is to attack and destroy wherever and whenever it can.

In the dark days of 1939 when Hitler's armies raped Poland, the world plunged into the horrors of the Second World War. At that time C.S. Lewis delivered an address to the students of Oxford University at the Church of St Mary. The text of that message became known as 'Learning in Wartime.' In the light of all that is happening today it has contemporary relevance:

> I think it is important to see the present calamity in a true perspective. The war creates no new situation; it simply aggravates the permanent human situation so that we can no longer ignore it. Human life has always been lived on the edge of a precipice … We are mistaken when we

compare war with 'normal life'. Life has never been normal
…

War makes death real to us: and that would have been
regarded as one of its blessings by most of the great
Christians of the past. They thought it good for us to be
always aware of our mortality. I am inclined to think they
were right. All the animal life in us, all schemes of happiness
that centred in this world, were always doomed to a final
destruction. In ordinary times only a wise man can realize
it. Now the stupidest of us knows. We see unmistakably the
sort of universe in which we have all along been living and
must come to terms with it. If we had foolish un-Christian
hopes about human culture, they are now shattered. If
we thought we were building up a heaven on earth, if we
looked for something that would turn the present world
from a place of pilgrimage into a permanent city satisfying
the soul of man, we are disillusioned, and not a moment
too soon.[1]

In the aftermath of 9/11 how can we, as believers, be helped
'to see the present calamity in a true perspective'? How can
we say to our fears that God is still in charge?

Immediately we face a fact that may seem both
uncomfortable and unpalatable. If, as Scripture teaches, God
is the Sovereign Lord of history, it follows that this world is
not at the mercy of blind fate. The logic of that statement is
clear. The devastation of the World Trade Centre happened,
and God did not intervene to stop it. He was not taken by
surprise. He allowed it to happen. Just as He allowed that
storm in Galilee to shake up His disciples' superficial view of
who He was. That may offend what someone has described

---

1. Lewis, C.S., *Learning in Wartime*; a sermon preached in the Church of St Mary
the Virgin, Oxford, autumn, 1939. https://bradleyggreen.com/attachments/
Lewis.Learning%20in%20War-Time.pdf Last accessed February 2020.

as 'the soft edges of our post-modern spirituality.' It certainly challenges a popularly held view of God in nominal Christian circles.

More than a decade ago the Berlin Wall fell. The bankruptcy of atheistic Communism was exposed. And we rejoiced. After all, in our book Communism was 'evil.' Smugly we congratulated ourselves that our democracies were 'good.' God, we said, was doing a new thing among the nations. The Sovereign Lord of History was on the move. And all the time, underlying our words, was an unspoken conviction that God must be 'on our side.' We are good – they are bad.

But what are we to say now? If God is on our side, how could He allow us to experience such suffering and devastation? It is an issue that raises more questions than answers. What will be the ongoing repercussions from this incident? How are we to view the upsurge of global terror and violence from radical idealists?

On what happened as the Twin Towers fell, many have been quick to offer their opinions. When on my hospital bed I heard one TV commentator say, 'Just think of it, the two symbols of our power and prosperity destroyed in one hour!' I wondered if he was consciously echoing the lament of the world's politicians as they witnessed the fall of Babylon in the book of Revelation. There, John records that seeing the smoke rising from the ruins world leaders cry out:

> Woe! Woe, O great city, O Babylon, city of power! In one hour your doom has come! (Rev. 18:10).

Was the TV commentator aware that in the aftermath of Babylon's doom, the businessmen would soon join the great lament of the politicians as the stock market plunged?

Woe! Woe, O great city, dressed in fine linen, purple and scarlet, and glittering with gold, precious stones and pearls! … In one hour such great wealth has been brought to ruin! (Rev. 18:16)

Did he see the impact this might have on the airlines and shipping companies as they joined in the chorus?

… all who travel by ship, the sailors, and all who earn their living from the sea, will stand far off. When they see the smoke of her burning, they will exclaim, 'Was there ever a city like this great city?' … They will throw dust on their heads, and with weeping and mourning cry out:

Woe! Woe to you, great city, where all who had ships on the sea became rich through her wealth! In one hour she has been brought to ruin! (Rev. 18:17-19).

The story of Babylon starts with the infamous tower of Babel (Gen. 11:1ff). The biblical significance of that first mention is hard to miss. Ronald Youngblood, the commentator on the text in the NIV Study Bible, writes:

At Babel rebellious man undertook a united and godless effort to establish for himself, by a titanic human enterprise, a world renown by which he would dominate God's creation.[2]

So Babylon, in all its proud luxury and glory, throughout Scripture comes to signify a culture of rebellion that puts its faith into its own efforts and stands up proudly in defiance against God, a kingdom that attempts by human effort to seize control of history.

In their pursuit of materialistic values, the economists, businessmen, along with the rest of us – the 'bodies and

---

2. NIV Study Bible, Genesis 11:4, Footnote.

souls of men,' (Rev. 18:13) are all entangled in the octopus-like tentacles of just such a Babylon. Yet, as history is drawn to a climax with the second coming of Christ, this proud materialistic self-sufficient culture will be shown to be bankrupt and will be ultimately destroyed (See Rev. 17–19). 'In one hour,' Babylon, all that symbolises the kingdom of man and his godless values, is to be thrown down. Then heaven will declare: 'The kingdom of the world has become the kingdom of our Lord and of his Christ, and he will reign for ever and ever' (Rev. 11:15).

Whatever else we could say, September 11th was a warning shot across the bow of our secular materialistic culture. Equally it challenges the kind of religion that develops within the nominal Church once the authority of Scripture has been eroded!

Now it would be a gross mistake to single out any one country and identify it with Babylon, whether it is in the West or the East. That would be to miss the deeper significance of biblical truth and repeat the same mistakes that have marked numerous attempts throughout church history to identify Babylon with the latest *bête noire*. Babylon is neither America nor Great Britain nor Russia, nor Iraq, nor Israel nor Iran, nor Beijing nor Jakarta, nor anywhere else in the world. Babylon is any man-made value system that ignores the rule of God. In that sense, Babylon manifests itself in the culture of each and every nation across the face of the globe. It is the manifestation of godlessness and rebellion against the authority of God and of His Christ, on a worldwide scale.

There are clear parallels with the symbolism of the book of Revelation. And we need to see that as a warning. A wake-up call. The spirit of Babylon is in all our hearts. It permeates all the cultures in which we live. By putting faith in our own achievements, and in ourselves, we reject the sovereignty of God. We are no longer moved to pray,

'Your kingdom come, your will be done, on earth as it is in heaven' (Matt. 6:10).

All this happened in New York, a city that, with some justification, proudly calls itself 'the world's capital.' It has given up some of its precious land to house the United Nations. It has great wealth and prosperity. It has become the major hub of the world's economy, sophisticated and prosperous. It has many remarkable achievements, not least of which is its ability to communicate instantly with the whole world.

From my hospital bed I witnessed the horrors within minutes of it taking place. Had it happened in some obscure corner of a remote country we might never have heard of it at all. But the trumpet has sounded a message round the whole earth, loud and clear, and none of us can say we have not heard it. World Babylon has been warned. A day is coming when it will be thrown down as Christ comes to reign. In the words of Joachim Neander's hymn:

> Human pride and earthly glory,
> sword and crown betray his trust;
> what with care and toil we fashion,
> tower and temple, fall to dust;
> but God's power,
> hour by hour
> is my temple and my tower.[3]

This universal message to the whole world challenges those who put their faith in the prosperity of their democracies. If the sovereign Lord of history exposed the bankruptcy of atheistic Communism, might he not now be exposing the bankruptcy of the practical atheism that some once so-

---

3. Neander, Joachim, 'God, My hope on you is founded', (1650–1680); translated from German by Robert S. Bridges.

called 'Christian' democracies have come to accept as the norm for their post-Christian 'way of life'?

Difficult and unpleasant though the thought may be, is God using the rise of global terror to challenge the growth of global secularisation and, at the same time, waken the Church? Is He exposing the bankruptcy of those popular humanist values that seek to destroy and push biblical Christian values to the margins of society? Not exactly what was expected after the collapse of the Berlin Wall! The emergence of global terror is a clear call to those of us who profess to follow Christ to re-evaluate our understanding of His ways. We must learn that holy reverence for Him and an understanding of His ways are the beginning of wisdom – the fear of the Lord.

In C.S. Lewis' book *The Lion, The Witch and The Wardrobe*, one of the four children at the Beavers' house said that she would feel nervous about meeting the Lion Aslan.

> Mrs Beaver said: 'That you will, dearie, and no mistake ... if there's anyone who can appear before Aslan without their knees knocking, they're either braver than most or else just silly.'
>
> 'Then he isn't safe?' said Lucy.
>
> 'Safe?' said Mr Beaver, 'Don't you hear what Mrs Beaver tells you? Who said anything about safe? Course he isn't safe. But he's good. He's the king, I tell you.'[4]

The prophet Habakkuk in the Old Testament knew all about knees knocking when God revealed what He was about to do by way of judgment on His own people. He had been on his knees praying for revival, sickened by the godless state

---

4. Lewis, C.S, *The Lion, the Witch and the Wardrobe* (New York City, NY: Harper Collins, 1950; p. 75.

of the nation. But God's answer was not what he bargained for. As he got up, his knees were most certainly knocking. His nation and people were in for a dreadful shock:

> Look at the nations and watch—and be utterly amazed. For I am going to do something in your days that you would not believe, even if you were told. I am raising up the Babylonians, that ruthless and impetuous people … (Hab. 1:5-6).

That was certainly not the answer he wanted or expected. It was terrifying. God was about to bring judgment on His people. God had answered his prayer in the depths, not the shallows. And as the truth of God's answer sank in Habakkuk was appalled:

> … O LORD, you have appointed them to execute judgment; O Rock, you have ordained them to punish (Hab. 1:12b).

The more he thought about it the more he had a theological problem. How could a holy God use the treachery of the evil Babylonian warriors whom he viewed to be terrorists, to deal with His own people who were nowhere near as evil as the Babylonians? Habakkuk cries out in protest:

> Your eyes are too pure to look on evil; you cannot tolerate wrong. Why then do you tolerate the treacherous? Why are you silent while the wicked swallow up those more righteous than themselves? (Hab. 1:13).

God's answer leaves as much unanswered as it answers. But one thing becomes crystal clear. Those who, like the Babylonians, resort to evil will in turn be consumed by the evil they choose to use. As Terry Waite, former adviser to the Archbishop of Canterbury and for several years taken hostage by terrorists in Lebanon, said: 'the terrible thing about terrorism is that ultimately it destroys those who practise it. Slowly but surely, as they try to extinguish life in others, the light within them dies.'[5]

Evil is true to its nature – it destroys. At the same time evil always exposes itself to the ultimate judgment of God. God sets its bounds.

Despite the evil, God remains holy and Habakkuk is called to hold on to the ultimate righteousness and goodness of God. That said, Habakkuk feels he has no way to fathom why God would allow evil men to wreak havoc on His nation. In their arrogance they have made evil a way of life. Habakkuk, in sharp contrast, eventually comes to understand that 'the righteous will live by his faith' (Hab. 2:4b). So it is by that faith he holds fast onto what he knows of God in the face of everything going on around him that seems so absolutely, mind bogglingly contradictory.

O Lord, are you not from everlasting? My God, my Holy One, we will not die (Hab. 1:12).

He holds on fast in faith to the fact that he knows God is still on the throne:

But the Lord is in his holy temple; let all the earth be silent before him (Hab. 2:20).

In faith he affirms that ultimately a day will come when:

… the earth will be filled with the knowledge of the glory of the Lord, as the waters cover the sea (Hab. 2:14).

---

5. Ratcliffe, Susan; Oxford Essential Quotations (4 Ed.); Oxford University Press; Published online 2016. Waite, Terry; 1939 – British religious adviser: in Guardian 20 February 1992.

In recognition of what is about to happen in his land he prays and pleads fervently:

> Lord ... I stand in awe of your deeds ... in wrath remember mercy (Hab. 3:2).

Habakkuk's final affirmation of faith shows us the mindset we need to cultivate in the face of the surge of the Global Terror phenomenon.

> I heard and my heart pounded,
> my lips quivered at the sound;
> decay crept into my bones, and my legs trembled.
> Yet I will wait patiently for the day of calamity
> to come on the nation invading us.
> Though the fig tree does not bud
> and there are no grapes on the vines,
> though the olive crop fails, and the fields produce no food,
> though there are no sheep in the pen
> and no cattle in the stalls,
> yet I will rejoice in the Lord,
> I will be joyful in God my Saviour.
> The Sovereign Lord is my strength; he makes my feet like the feet
> of a deer, he enables me to go on the heights (Hab. 3:16-9).

Living in the Southern kingdom of Judah, Habakkuk knew that Israel in the North had faced judgement, when she ignored her calling to be God's servant. God had called His people to be salt and light to the nations. He had given them many warnings.

Israel failed. Instead of bearing witness to God's glory she gave herself to a preoccupation with the formal rituals of religion. It compromised with worshiping other gods. Their calling, to be a 'light to the nations' (Isa. 49:6 GNT). was so distorted that the light of their testimony was extinguished. The prophet Hosea warned them that by their disobedience they were sowing the wind and would 'reap the whirlwind' (Hos. 8:7).

That whirlwind came with the Assyrian conquest. God called these Assyrians 'the rod of my anger, in whose hand is the club of my wrath' (Isa. 10:5). The warning ignored, the Northern Kingdom disappeared. To this day the people of that region are remembered as the Ten Lost Tribes of Israel. A warning and example we should not ignore.

Jesus made it equally clear to us that we are to be salt and light. He commissioned us as His disciples to make disciples of all nations. He expects us to obey that commission. However, the undermining of the authority of Scripture and the decline of gospel truth in nominal churches suggests that in some countries, once considered 'Christian,' at least nominally, the light of a gospel testimony has all but disappeared – the moral decay and breakdown of family life being clear evidence of the all-pervasive and corrosive spirit of Babylon.

The voice of Christian conscience is all but silent in the corridors of power in our Western democracies. The non-Christian world today hears more of the technical innovation, commercial enterprise and moral depravity of the West rather than the gospel of grace. Apart from a few committed individuals, the missionary vision of the church and its motivation for World mission is in danger of being eclipsed in the nominal church by a navel-gazing preoccupation with its own interests.

Many of the civilising Christian values that once helped to shape the nations and international institutions of our modern world owe much historically to the worldwide propagation of the gospel. Fundamental truths and values derived from the gospel helped shape moral behaviour and undergird what are now internationally accepted standards of justice, equality and civil behaviour. But if the Church, called to be salt and light, is now in two minds about submitting to the authority of Scripture, and if the great commission to preach the gospel is being overlooked, then failure to accept and submit to the authority of God's Word will, in turn, undermine the structure and stability of the civilised world. And that may well prove to be a more destructive threat to world peace than the enrichment of uranium and the acquisition of nuclear weapons.

As followers of Christ, His Church, His household, we must not ignore Peter's warning ' … it is time for judgment to begin with the family of God; and if it begins with us, what will the outcome be for those who do not obey the gospel of God?'(1 Pet. 4:17). Recent events and the rise of Global Terror call us to repentance and challenge us to a missionary concern for the nations.

Our knees may knock as we think of all that is happening, but our faith needs the confidence expressed in Joachim Neander's hymn:

> All my hope on God is founded,
> All my trust he shall renew,
> He, my guide through changing order,
> Only good and only true:
> God unknown,
> He alone
> Calls my heart to be his own.[6]

Only then will we be helped to begin 'to see the present calamity in a true perspective.'

---

6. Neander, Joachim, 'All my hope on God is founded'; translated from German by Robert S. Bridges, 1899.

CHAPTER 5

Riots, Religion or Repentance

… the line dividing good and evil cuts through the heart of every human being, and who among us is willing to destroy a piece of their own heart?
– Solzhenitsyn

Jakarta was tense. It was election time. A phone call from Switzerland brought us the news that Richard Bachman's father had passed away. Political demonstrations and election fever or not, I knew I had to drive the VW minibus out to the University where he was teaching to break the news and pray with him and his wife Elisabeth.

On my way home the Jakarta Bypass was eerily quiet. One or two army tanks were out and about. Something did not feel right. Then, as I turned off the bypass into Jalan Suprapto, suddenly, right in front of me, was a burning bus. Mobs of rioters everywhere.

I was in the grip of fear. Smoke, flames, a mob wielding knives and sticks. A human tidal wave enveloping everything in its path. There was no escape. Half a mile from home, trapped behind the wheel of my car. No way forward. No way back.

It was election time. All the diverse political parties were rioting. I could feel the rush of adrenalin. An estimated mob of around a million militants with election fever were running amok through the streets of Jakarta hijacked by anarchist elements intent on looting and burning like a swarm of angry locusts, leaving devastation behind them. Our Mission Home was in their path.

Instinctively I pushed the door lock of my VW Combi with my elbow and wound up the window. Smoke from burning shops dimmed the evening light. Cars and trucks were on fire. Flames roared from a row of bus windows a few yards from my door. Youths, shirts tied at the waist, with their headbands making them look like pirates, were rocking the car in front of my bumper. The driver was dragged out onto the road.

Then the sickening thud of hands trying to rock my van. It began to sway. Angry eyes peering at the windows. Three or four rioters hung from the roof gutter. I was next for the turn and burn routine. They tried the doors, but they were locked. I had seconds.

With clarity born in crisis I sensed, rather than saw, the empty grass verge. Further on, a strip of asphalt led to factory gates. The Coca-Cola plant. The gates were shut. The guards were armed. It was that or nothing.

Letting the clutch in, I shot across the grass. My would-be assailants fell off. But in the half-light of evening the sudden violence of my approach created a problem for the guards. Was this a rioter about to crash the gates? Should they shoot? I screeched to a halt within inches. And as I braked, stones were hurled at the van. Ominous noises as they hit the tailgate. The truth must have dawned on the gatekeepers. Seeing my white face, they probably mistook me for one of their expat staff. One of the gates was opened just wide enough for me to negotiate the chicane into the factory. I had bought time.

I could see in my mirror guards rushing to lock the gates before the mob entered. There was shooting. I gained as much distance as I could. Parking out of sight behind a large warehouse, I ran inside.

There in a small room was a crowd of frightened factory workers huddled together. The heat was oppressive. No electricity, no fans, no light, just a quiet atmosphere of fear. Together we sat hushed and still in darkness – the air heavy with the unmistakable smell of burning cloves from their kretek cigarettes. How long did we have?

Twilight gave way to darkness. People came and went. An injured man, his left arm slashed and pouring blood, staggered into the room. Immediately friends ran to help. It was not clear where he had come from. But as each newcomer arrived, they added to the jigsaw of our understanding of what was going on beyond the gates.

I could hardly dare to imagine what must have happened to our offices and Mission Home. Just half a mile down the road, OMF's Mission Home stuck out like a sore thumb. A prime target for the violence. What if Adèle and all the others had been attacked? I had to get back.

One man came into the room with an air of authority. A factory foreman perhaps? He began to tell us of the shooting and looting he had seen. He seemed so sure that I plucked up courage to ask: 'What about Ricoh House?'

This was the name given to the buildings next door to our Mission Home.

'Finished! Burned out! Totally destroyed!'

With the heavy emphasis and explosive syllables of an authentic Javanese speaker, each word sent a shiver down my spine.

Of course, I knew I shouldn't be so afraid. I knew chapter and verse by heart that I was in God's hands. But this was a concrete reality. People were being killed. Real blood was being spilled. The sharp cracks you could hear were from real rifles. This wasn't TV. It was happening, and I was trapped in it all. The irrational mobs were intent on mayhem. And the news that the place where everyone I loved had been destroyed made me sick with fear. How could this be happening and how could God let my family suffer?

I told myself there was nothing to fear but fear, but the knot in my stomach tightened. I had to get back to see for myself – riots or no riots. The van would have to stay. It would probably get stolen or burned, but there was no way to drive through a rioting mob. It would be suicide. If only I wasn't so conspicuous. A large white Caucasian was hardly likely to go unnoticed picking his way through a sea of Indonesian rioters. But I had to do something. I moved to the door but as I tried to leave, a man stood in the doorway. My way was blocked.

He had the air of someone who expected to be obeyed. He wore the little white hat that indicated he had made the pilgrimage to Mecca. He was a Hajji. I was determined to try and get out; but as I made to go past him, he shot out a hand and grabbed my arm. His grip, firm but kindly. Aware of my fear, he spoke calmly:

'Don't be afraid! Stay still. It's not time yet. Later – I will take you. Patience, Tuan.'

I deferred – it meant another two hours – an eternity. I talked with the others squatting around the edge of the room. They were every bit as afraid as I was. They soon discovered that I was a Christian missionary – there are no secrets in Asia. They were as kind and polite as they could be irrespective of whatever their political or religious persuasions might have been. Their concern for what might have happened to my family was genuine. Circumstances had thrown us together. We found a common bond in our shared crisis.

Gradually the noises on the street quietened. My Hajji friend slipped out of the room to see if the coast was clear. A few minutes later he returned and beckoned. Then, in the way Indonesian men seem able to hold another man's hand without embarrassment, he gripped my hand and just held tight. Hand in hand, we stepped out into the humid tropical night.

Our path was lit by flames from the burning vehicles. The air was full of the acrid smell of burning rubber. Yet it felt fresh after that stuffy room. We crossed the factory yard to thread our way through the shadowy back streets of the housing estate. Past the local hospital and finally out onto the main road. Rioters were still wandering around with sticks, prodding at the burning vehicles. Skirting a fence, we moved towards a pyre of burning cars and buses. They were to the side of the Mission Home in front of the shops. No wonder our foreman thought the buildings had been burned out and destroyed. From the road, that was certainly how it looked. I felt devastated and hollow.

The burning vehicles created a sense of confusion. Yet, as my eyes adjusted to the smoke and flames, I saw that the Mission Home, far from standing out like the sore thumb, had all but disappeared. The lights were off. One of our team, Anne Lea, who had seen me off in the VW several hours ago, was standing waiting by the gate. But there was something else. In the darkness, the glare of light from the burning vehicles flickered on the trees in the garden. And the eye was deceived. A curtain of light seemed to hide the building. Unless you knew it to be there it was almost invisible. By the grace of God, the mobs had ignored it and gone to loot the lucrative shops next door. Adèle was safe along with all the other missionaries. They had gathered to pray. Their prayers had been answered.

My worthy guide brought me right into the Mission Home. He wouldn't let go of my hand until he could pass it safely over to Adèle. He took a quick drink of tea and then when we sought to reward him in some way for bringing me through the riots, he refused. Slipping quietly out through the darkness of our garden into the light of the burning vehicles next door he disappeared and was gone. A good man – for me, at that moment – an angel unawares.

It was a scary time. With National Elections two weeks away. Extremists on every side were bent on chaos. But that night, identified in fear with a frightened group of Indonesians hiding in the warehouse, I was given a lot to think about. They showed genuine concern and compassion – one of them risking his life for a total stranger whose background and beliefs were so very different from his own.

How easy it is to pass judgement on those who do not share our beliefs and convictions. There in the oppressive heat of that dark room some of my assumptions were challenged. You find the good, the bad and the ugly in every group no matter what label it wears. We are so often quick to see the views and beliefs of others through our own set of distorting mirrors but all too slow to accept that we often fail to understand how others may see us.

One day the famous Scottish poet, Robert Burns, was sitting comfortably in church. He was behind a pious lady who was wearing a bonnet trimmed beautifully with ribbons and bows. He was fascinated. Then suddenly, crawling through the decorations he saw one of her head lice. He was struck by the sheer incongruity of it all – the demure lady, prim and proper sitting piously in church, totally oblivious of the louse on her bonnet. Little could she have known that one of her head lice would give birth to some of his most famous lines:

> O wad some Power the giftie gie us
> To see oursels as ithers see us!
> It wad frae monie a blunder free us,
> An' foolish notion:[1]

Burns probably found the incongruity of the louse more interesting than the sermon, but through his art a sermon lives on.

If as followers of Christ we want to avoid 'monie a blunder' in our relationship with men and women who do not share our faith, we need to understand how they may view the 'Christian' bonnet that adorns the Church and indeed our own heads as followers of Christ. Sometimes the ribbons and lace are crawling alive with a great deal that is off-putting to say the least. Not a pretty sight.

Many years later than those riots in Jakarta and just very recently in London I was at a funeral and got a taste of how someone saw some of 'the lice on our bonnet.' The service had ended. The close family members were away from the church to the crematorium. A good number of us awaited their return to join those of us staying back at the church. Tea and sandwiches had been provided. We were busy helping ourselves to finger food and chatting. Making new acquaintances.

The young woman who had passed away was my daughter-in-law Joyce's older sister. She was a believer. The

---

1. English Translation:
   'Oh would some Power give us the gift,
   To see ourselves as others see us!
   It would from many a blunder free us,
   And foolish notion:'

minister, who knew her well, gave the clearest of gospel messages with a winsome sensitivity. Some of those waiting for the family to return were not Christians. Quite a few were friends and colleagues from her workplace; her life and witness had affected them. She had shown them much love and was greatly loved and admired in return.

One of her friends, whom I had never met before, approached and the subject of the minister's message became the subject of our conversation.

'And what did you think about what the minister said?' I asked.

'Oh, I am not religious.'

'And why is that?'

'I once went along to a church for three years but it was all: thou shalt not smoke; thou shalt not drink; thou shalt not dance; thou shalt not have sex before marriage; and worse, some of the so-called leaders were caught leading a double life – they were just complete hypocrites – so I left!'

I'm not surprised he left. I didn't blame him. I might probably have done the same. Sadly, the kind of religion he encountered drove him away from Christ, no matter it was dressed up in pious Christian terminology. He seemed unable to hear the clear message of the gospel of grace the minister had explained so well. Tragic if those looking on at the Church find living faith fossilised into an off-putting religion of do's and don'ts!

If you once displace the central gospel (the good news) of the love of God and His saving grace in Christ with a set of religious sounding practices, it becomes an aggressive cancer. And like cancer, it will eat away the life and witness of a church. It eats corrosively from within. The fellowship dies and desiccates like a dead cockroach lying on its back with its feet in the air. The Pharisees and Sadducees, who crucified Christ, were all devoutly religious. It was their religion that drove them to hate and reject the very one who had come to be their Saviour.

As my conversation with this good man at the funeral continued, he added yet another argument which I think he thought would justify his not being, as he put it, 'not very religious.'

'All this upsurge of terrorism and violence that is going on today is caused by religion,' he ventured.

'What then about Genghis Khan? Hitler? Stalin? Pol Pot? Mao Tse Tung ... would you call them religious?'

My question pulled him up for a moment. We may not like it, but the nominal 'Religion' of Christianity, as history shows, does indeed have a lot to answer for. There is much blood in our own backyard. But to go along with the notion that religion is the root cause of all the violence in our world today is a superficial misunderstanding. The factors that give rise to revolutionary terrorism and the use of violence go far deeper, the root and stem lying deep within the human heart.

In the words of Vishal Mangalwadi, one of India's foremost Christian intellectuals:

> The fallacy of Revolutionary idealism usually lies in its mistaken assumption that the root of the human problem lies in socio-political structures and not in the human being and 'Religion' can so often, in fact, be little more than just another socio-political man-made structure that is powerless to solve the human problem.[2]

'Religion' is a system designed and created by man; 'little more than ... a socio-political man-made structure.''Religion'

2. Vishal Mangalwadi, LLD, born and raised in India studied eastern religion and philosophy in India, Hindu ashrams, and at L'Abri Fellowship in Switzerland. He is a social reformer, political columnist, one of India's foremost Christian intellectuals.

in that sense is not a word the Bible treats with any sympathy. Indeed, Jesus reserved His fiercest denunciations for the hypocrisy of such religion. After all, it was religion that put Him on the cross.

The famous Swiss theologian, Karl Barth, puts his finger on the issue when in his 'Church Dogmatics' he made the daring statement:

'Religion is unbelief ... [and] ... the one great concern of godless humanity.'

By 'Religion,' Barth was speaking of it being a system of ideas, rules and regulations designed by man as a way to God; a human construct; a self-made system of rituals created on earth as a way to heaven. Something that is a million miles away from the gospel of God's grace where God Himself in Christ took the initiative to make us right with Himself; reconciling us to Himself by way of the cross.

> The Word was God ... The Word became flesh and made his dwelling among us. We have seen his glory, the glory of the one and only Son, who came from the Father, full of grace and truth (John 1:1, 14).

As Tim Keller says:

> The founders of every other major religion said, 'I'm a prophet who shows you how to find God,' but Jesus taught, 'I'm God, come to find you.' This means we can't look at Jesus as only one more religious teacher supplementing the world's store of wisdom. He was either a conscious fraud, was himself deluded, or was in fact divine. Duncan[3] called this a trilemma.[4]

---

3. 'Rabbi' John Duncan (1796-1870) and C.S. Lewis.

4. Keller, Timothy; *Encounters with Jesus*; Hodder and Stoughton; 2013; isbn 9781444754155; page 45 (Kindle Edition).

Vishal Mangalwadi sees it from another perspective:

> God became man in order to save man, because man was made in God's image – precious and immortal. Full implications of these doctrines are still being worked out. Yet, much of our future will be shaped by the question: Is man merely another animal (organic intelligence) or is he uniquely God's image—so precious to God that He would come to this earth to save him?[5]

The Russian novelist, Alexander Solzhenitsyn, lying in a Siberian prison camp, had his presuppositions challenged as he witnessed some appalling and dehumanizing horrors. In his book, *The Gulag Archipelago,* he wrote:

> It was only when I lay there on rotting prison straw that I sensed within myself the first stirrings of good. Gradually it was disclosed to me that the line separating good and evil passes not through states, nor between classes, nor between political parties either, but right through every human heart, and through all human hearts. This line shifts. Inside us, it oscillates with the years …

Evil is not a problem of Communism nor is it the problem of capitalism or any of our religions – it is my problem. As Paul put it: 'All have sinned and come short of the glory of God' (Rom. 3:23 KJV). That is a universal truth for 'the heart is deceitful above all things and beyond cure. Who can understand it?'(Jer. 17:9). The corruption of the human heart is what lies at the root of the problem. The more we suppress that truth the more unpredictably it will erupt and

---

5. From an interview about his book, *The Book That Made Your World: How the Bible Created the Soul of Western Civilization*; Thomas Nelson; 2012. See https://www.biblegateway.com/blog/2015/07/how-the-bible-created-the-soul-of-western-civilization-an-interview-with-vishal-mangalwadi/

surprise us with devastating results. Evil, left unchecked, will destroy. That is its nature. It is in its DNA.

At a personal level as well as at the national level our only escape from the hold of evil is to turn from it in repentance. Jesus died to save us from evil and taught us to pray: 'Lead us not into temptation but deliver us from the evil one' (Matt. 6:13, Gal. 1:4). A prayer to turn daily from evil and open ourselves up to God.

When the tower of Siloam fell, and innocent people died, Jesus gave us the same message:

> Those eighteen who died when the tower in Siloam fell on them—do you think they were more guilty than all the others living in Jerusalem? I tell you, no! But unless you repent, you too will all perish (Luke 13:4-5).

Repentance involves radical surgery. It is both difficult and painful. In Solzhenitsyn's words:

> If only there were evil people out there, insidiously committing evil deeds, and it was only necessary to separate them from the rest of us and destroy them! But the line dividing good and evil cuts through the heart of every human being, and who among us is willing to destroy a piece of their own heart?[6]

---

6. Solzhenitsyn, Aleksandr, *The Gulag Archipelago*. https://www.goodreads.com/quotes/1020045-if-only-there-were-evil-people-somewhere-insidiously-committing-evil Last accessed February 2020.

CHAPTER 6

The God who Suffers

… to our wounds only God's wounds can speak.
– Edward Shillito

Thomas Hamilton was a man with a grudge. He had run boys' clubs. The local community was suspicious. They banned the clubs. And they were right. His interest in young boys was far from wholesome.

Dunblane, a prosperous commuter town in the central belt of Scotland, was a close-knit community. It was a cold Wednesday morning in March. Fathers had left for work. Mothers had wrapped their children warmly against the cold. The early morning hustle and bustle of breakfast behind them, the children had been bundled off to school. Just another day. Classes had barely begun when Hamilton strode through the school and joined the children in the gym. It was a place he knew. It was where he had held his boys' clubs.

Mrs. Gwenne Mayor had the children of Primary-One well organised. They were laughing and playing happily. From under his anorak, Hamilton reached for one of his four pistols. One by one he emptied them, picking off the children as they huddled in a corner around their teacher. In less than three minutes sixteen of the infants along with their teacher lay dead or dying. Then finally Hamilton turned the gun on himself. Twelve other children lay badly injured, along with the two teachers who had rushed in to help. Our five-year-old niece, Mhairi, was one of those who died.

Emergency teams confronted the scene of carnage. Dead and dying children lay on the floor. John McEwan of the Forth Valley Ambulance service described the horror: 'It was not so much the dying; it was five-year-old children looking unbelievingly at bullet holes in their arms and legs, and who could not comprehend what was happening ... the very fact that they were Primary-One children meant that words couldn't begin to describe it ... it was macabre, grotesque and disgusting.'

Like any other little girl, our niece was a bright and lively five-year-old. But she had a special role in the family. Her father had only recently died. So, she was growing up to be a companion for her mother, Isabel, and three-month-old baby sister Catherine. Her father, Murray, a lecturer in philosophy in the Department of Religious Studies at Stirling University, had just died at the age of forty-eight. He was not to see the birth of his second child. In a uniquely tragic way, his memorial service was to have taken place that very afternoon at Stirling University.

After the memorial service in Dunblane Cathedral, I conducted the service for Mhairi at the same crematorium where just six months before I had taken her father's funeral. Immediately after the service I headed to Heathrow and my flight back to Singapore. Knowing why I had to delay my flight by a day, Singapore Airlines had deferred my ticket.

In normal circumstances I have no trouble sleeping on the overnight flight. I had done it many times before. This time, with great consideration, the airline had allocated three special seats so that I could 'stretch out and sleep' for the thirteen-hour journey. Three seats or no three seats, I did not sleep.

As I had boarded the plane, there in the magazine rack was a copy of Newsweek. The cover was a full-page black and white picture of Mhairi staring at me from her class photograph. And all I could think was: WHY? Why the senseless killing of innocents? Why didn't God intervene to stop it all?

In the face of such stark tragedy, many journalists wrote at great length, saying that there are no words to be written. Even to speak of tragedy, one said, is to use a word devalued by overuse. All true. As I sat, I went over and over the funeral service. The reading of Scripture would have brought some comfort but, apart from that, I wondered what else could have been said in the face of such suffering. The agony of loss to a young mother still grieving for her husband. I was hurting – what must she have felt?

How was it vaguely possible for her 'to see the present calamity in a true perspective?' We believe that God is good. We believe He is love. We believe that He is Sovereign. Then, in the words of Rabbi Harold Kushner, 'Why do bad things happen to good people?' If God is love, and God is good and all-powerful, then the existence of evil and our experience of suffering mean we are facing ultimate and unanswerable questions.

With heightened international tensions and rumours of terrorism, we are being forced to ask questions that we would rather not have to think about. And when we become victims, marshmallow ideas we may have been fed about God, as if He were some benign eternal Santa Claus, will do little to help us cope with so intense a pain. Ultimately, whatever perspectives bring us a degree of relief, we are going to have to face the truth spelled out in Paul's great doxology:

> Oh, the depth of the riches of the wisdom and knowledge
> of God! How unsearchable his judgments, and his paths
> beyond tracing out! Who has known the mind of the Lord?
> Or who has been his counsellor? (Rom. 11:33-34)

We still look for whatever light we can find. We remind ourselves that God chose to make us the way we are. He knew the limitations we would face. He did not create us to be robots. We are not clones. And when He made us, He did not choose to make us immune to suffering. Daringly He made us in His image. He chose to give us the freedom of choice – with all that the entire gift involved. For with the gift came the freedom to choose good and the freedom to choose evil. The freedom to obey, the freedom to disobey, the freedom to delight in the law of God, the freedom to walk in the counsel of the ungodly, (Ps. 1), even the freedom to ignore His very existence and live our own way without any reference to Him. Freedom carries consequences. And God knew before He even created the world that it would involve suffering. So, when God created us to have the freedom of choice, He did so knowing all the suffering and pain that would arise from our making wrong choices.

The fact that God knew about suffering in His world becomes clearer when we remember that Jesus was active in the creation of our world:

> ... For by him all things were created: things in heaven and
> on earth, visible and invisible, whether thrones or powers
> or rulers or authorities; all things were created by him and
> for him. He is before all things, and in him all things hold
> together (Col. 1:15-17).

And hard though it may be to fathom, the cross and all that was involved was in the mind of God from the dawn of time.

The book of Revelation tells us that the one by whom and for whom all things were created was also 'the Lamb that was slain from the creation of the world' (Rev. 13:8).

Our salvation was in the mind of God before He ever said, 'Let there be light.' And He chose us in Christ: 'before the creation of the world to be holy and blameless in his sight. In love he predestined us to be adopted as his sons through Jesus Christ' (Eph. 1:4-5). So He knew. And He knew at the same time that He would experience suffering more than any of us would ever know.

When God sent His Son into our world, He was not wrapped in sanitised cotton wool. He came to a germ-laden cattle trough. While the shepherds on the hills may have enjoyed the angelic choir recital, at street level the singing would soon be replaced with the screams of distraught mothers, agonising for their slaughtered babies. Christ was born into a world of suffering. Light years removed from the sentimentalised images on our Christmas cards.

God is not indifferent. He identifies with our suffering. And He does so without in any way compromising His love or omnipotence. The suffering-love of God binds together two facts of life that are inseparable in our experience. Where there is love there will be suffering. The tension between love and suffering may be beyond the reach of my reason, but that is not to say it is against reason.

Suffering we know. But what do we really mean by love? The word has become debased. It is this that makes it more difficult for us to reconcile suffering with love. Here we can only turn again to the cross – where the justice and wrath of God combine with His love and mercy as He suffers. There at the foot of that cross, while we may not have answers, we are drawn to the only appropriate response – humble worship. For there we see that our God suffers. The only appropriate response I can make is to bow before His cross and say with Job: 'My ears had heard of you but now my eyes have seen you. Therefore I despise myself and repent in dust and ashes' (Job 42:5-6).

God is no stranger to suffering – He has experienced it for everyone (Heb. 2:9). Bishop James Jones in his book, *Why Do People Suffer?* tells the poignant story of a school which collapsed in an earthquake:

> A school had caved in, killing all the teachers and most of the children.
>
> A little boy, badly maimed, was rescued from the rubble and rushed to hospital. For hours a team of doctors and nurses fought to save his life while his mother waited anxiously inside the operating theatre. After seven hours of painstaking surgery the little boy died.
>
> Instead of leaving it to the nurse to tell the mother, the surgeon went himself. As he broke the dreadful news the mother became hysterical in her grief and attacked the surgeon, pummelling his chest with her fists. But instead of pushing her away, the doctor held her to himself tightly until the woman's sobbing subsided and she rested cradled in his arms.
>
> And then in the heavy silence the surgeon began to weep. Tears streamed down his face and grief racked his body. For he had come to the hospital the moment he heard that his one and only son had been killed in the same school.[1]

Grief, anger, pain, we experience them all in suffering. And while we may not be able to say so openly, deep down we can even get angry with God. At such a time He would hold us tightly if only we will let Him. He, more than anyone, knows

---

1. Jones, James, *Why Do People Suffer?* (Oxford: Lion Hudson, 2007), pp. 54-56.

just what we are going through. 'For God so loved the world that he gave his one and only Son, that whoever believes in him shall not perish but have eternal life' (John 3:16).

The godly Archbishop William Temple once observed that people say there cannot be a God of love: '... because if there was, and he looked upon the world, his heart would break. The church points to the cross and says, "It did break."'

John Stott, in his book, *The Cross of Christ*, strikes a chord that rings true to those of us who have spent a great part of our lives on the foreign mission field. He says:

> In the real world of pain, how could one worship a God who was immune to it? I have entered many Buddhist temples in different Asian countries and stood respectfully before the statue of the Buddha, his legs crossed, arms folded, eyes closed, the ghost of a smile playing round his mouth, a remote look on his face, detached from the agonies of the world. But each time, after a while I have had to look away. And in imagination I have turned instead to the lonely, twisted, tortured figure on the cross, nails through hands and feet, back lacerated, limbs wrenched, brow bleeding from thorn pricks, mouth dry and intolerably thirsty, plunged in God-forsaken darkness. That is the God for me! He laid aside His immunity to pain. He entered our world of flesh and blood, tears and death. He suffered for us. Our sufferings become more manageable in the light of His. There is still a question mark against human suffering, but over it we stamp another mark, the cross which symbolizes divine suffering.[2]

In 1983, Eric Wolterstorff, an experienced young climber, fell to his death in a climbing accident in Austria. Eric was

---

2. Stott, John R. W., *The Cross of Christ* (London: IVP, 1987), pp. 335-336.

in his prime. A young life cut off at twenty-five years. Eric was deeply loved and mourned by his father whose sense of loss was intense. His father Nicholas wrote of his grief in his 'Lament for a Son':

> God is love. That is why he suffers. To love our suffering, sinful world is to suffer. God so suffered for the world that he gave up his only Son to suffering. The one who does not see God's suffering does not see his love. God is suffering love. So suffering is down at the centre of things, deep down where the meaning is. Suffering is the meaning of our world. For love is the meaning. And love suffers. The tears of God are the meaning of history.

And while that does not answer all our questions, it sheds light into the appalling darkness of suffering. Wolterstoff found he still had a mystery on his hands. He continues:

> But mystery remains: Why isn't Love-without-suffering the meaning of things? Why is suffering-Love the meaning? Why does God endure his suffering? Why does he not at once relieve his agony by relieving ours?[3]

To that heart cry there can be no clinical response. Yet by looking at the cross we find perspective in God's revelation of Himself as the God who suffers. Like Job we can only say through the mystery, 'My ears had heard of you but now my eyes have seen you' (Job 42:5). Job did not arrive at a set of neat answers despite the strenuous efforts of his 'expert' counsellors. But in the light of God's self-revelation some of the fog lifted enough for him to do the only thing that he, and any of us, can do – he worshipped.

---

3. Wolterstorff, Nicholas, *Lament for a Son* (Grand Rapids, MI: William B. Eermans, 1987), p. 90.

The Rev Edward Shillito ministered at a church just outside London early in the last century. He was moved by the appalling sufferings of those whose bodies were grotesquely maimed and disfigured in the battles of the First World War. As he visited and saw their suffering he grappled with issues of faith. His struggles were poured out in the many poems he wrote. One that has been frequently quoted is addressed to the 'Jesus of the Scars' – the crucified suffering Christ who showed His wounds to His disciples. It ends with these moving words:

> … Lord Jesus, by Thy Scars we claim Thy grace.
>
> If when the doors are shut, Thou drawest near,
> Only reveal those hands, that side of Thine;
> We know to-day what wounds are, have no fear,
> Show us Thy Scars, we know the countersign.
> The other gods were strong; but Thou wast weak;
> They rode, but Thou didst stumble to a throne;
> But to our wounds only God's wounds can speak,
> And not a god has wounds, but Thou alone.[4]

To the mocking question, 'where is your God?'

When we face pain beyond expression, we do not have all the answers. But we have a God with wounds.

---

4. Shillito, Edward, 'Jesus of the Scars', 1919.

CHAPTER 7

The God who Reigns

I believe in Christianity as I believe that the sun has risen: not only because I see it, but because by it I see everything else. –
C. S. Lewis

It was Christmas. We were in Central Java. Alongside our work with the Javanese Church, both of us taught at a Christian university. Our students presented us with an unusual Christmas card – a banner strung across the street immediately outside our front gate. It had an unusual greeting:

> The spirit of Christmas demands that we kick to death all Colonial Imperialist dogs.

At one end of the bold red lettering stood a crudely painted Union Jack. At the other, the Stars and Stripes. John Bull and Uncle Sam, looking greedy and covered with dollar signs, added an artistic flourish. Not your run-of-the mill Santa Claus and jingle bells Christmas card!

This vocabulary was everywhere during the years of President Sukarno's Revolution. The banner had been hung there by Christian students from the University. With the inscrutable polite courtesy of the Javanese, they had asked our permission to put it outside our gate. They were at great pains to assure us it was nothing personal. They did not want us to feel offended.

Poor souls, they had an identity crisis and our presence, as Westerners in their University, did not help them. We were, after all, representatives from a nation that enjoyed the most hated nation status in their latest propaganda war. It would have been hard for them to understand that perhaps we could feel just a little threatened by their Christmas banner. But then, we had to try and understand the problem from their point of view. We did what we could and invited them in for Christmas cake; they left most of it uneaten. Evidently too sweet by Javanese standards! As one of students put it to our great amusement, 'It's good I've got a strong stomach, or I would have been sick!'

The communists were strong. Indonesia, under Soekarno, was pursuing an anti-colonialist revolution. The USA was at war in Vietnam to the North and it was an atrocious mess. The so-called 'domino theory' predicted that before long Indonesia would also fall to Communism. And any Christian student who did not show enthusiastic support for 'the Revolution' against colonial imperialists was suspect. So, our Christian brothers and sisters had to chant the latest political shibboleths as loudly as they could, to avoid the accusation of being unpatriotic.

It really looked as if Indonesia was about to become a communist country. Who was to know then that a coup d'état launched by the Communist party the following year was to be thwarted? At the time it was hard not to believe they would succeed. Britain was in the process of helping Malaya, Sarawak, and Borneo, along with Singapore, to form a new nation to be called Malaysia. That, in Indonesian government propaganda, was a neo-colonialist plot orchestrated by Britain to break up the 'Jakarta – Phnom Penh – Hanoi – Beijing' axis of the NEFOS

(The 'New Emerging Forces'). At that point of time, as Brits, we were not popular.

Nor was our Embassy. It stood to one side of a great roundabout opposite the Hotel Indonesia. A great seething mass of humanity gathered there to hurl their insults and demand an audience with the British ambassador.

In his wisdom and years of experience in the diplomatic service, the ambassador realised that he couldn't negotiate with a mob. So, he produced his secret weapon – a Scottish soldier complete with bagpipes.

Our brave Scot was later to be given a medal for his courage for what seemed to us to be nothing but an act of diplomatic folly. He marched up and down in front of the embassy and released all the pent-up power of the pipes. The result was predictable. The rampaging mobs burnt the embassy down. There is a time and place for the pipes – the ramparts of Edinburgh Castle, the mountainside or the city square. But the British Embassy in Jakarta, in tropical heat and before rioting mobs, was neither the time nor the place.

I had to go to Jakarta to visit the temporary consulate that replaced the burnt-out embassy. The British ambassador had been withdrawn and a skeleton staff remained. I met the consul. His advice was, in a word: 'Get out – leave the country!'

I remembered a recent conversation with the Principal of the Christian University, in whose house I had been living.

'Would you be better off if we left? Are we a danger to you, staying here on campus?'

He had taken his time to answer. When it came, it was very moving.

'Yes, of course it would be better. Better for you. Better for us. As Christians in Central Java we have an identity crisis. We are a minority hemmed in by elements of our own culture on one side and the political philosophy of Communism on the other. But you and I are brothers in Christ. You identify with us and take the consequences and we will identify with you. We are all members of one family in Christ.'

Given that bond, my answer to the consul was clear.

'Thank you, but we have decided to stay put.'

At that the consul became angry.

'When I give advice to businessmen, they follow it. You missionaries give me more trouble than anyone else! You think God will take care of you. Now you are on your own. Is that understood?'

It was. He had a job to do. He was acting in what he felt were our best interests. We were choosing to ignore his advice. He had to protect himself. We did not blame him. But given the nature of our relationship with the Javanese Church, in Luther's words, it was a case of 'Here I stand, I can do no other. So, help me God!'

It was then that the BBC Far Eastern service began to send hourly broadcasts to all British citizens in Indonesia. We tuned in to the shortwave radio to keep up to date with the news. The RAF was sending Hercules aircraft to Jakarta to evacuate all UK citizens. We were told to make our way to the airport and take a plane out to Singapore. It was tempting. Life in Java in the early sixties was far from comfortable, and it was hard not to be fearful.

All day we had been listening for instructions as to what we should do as foreigners. That night it was our weekly prayer meeting and we were working systematically through Isaiah for our Bible readings. High on our agenda as we came to prayer was, how should we respond to the advice we were being given? In our Bible readings it 'just so happened' that we had come to Isaiah 31.

> Woe to those who go down to Egypt for help, who rely on horses, who trust in the multitude of their chariots and in the great strength of their horsemen, but do not look to the Holy One of Israel, or seek help from the LORD ... But the Egyptians are men and not God; their horses are flesh and not spirit. (Isa. 31:1-3)

Israel was being warned against a military alliance with Egypt. Egypt had all the latest military equipment by way of fine horses and chariots. It would have been tempting for Israel to place an order for the latest form of Egyptian armaments. But the message was clear. If she put her trust in God, He would not let her down. After all, it was God, not the government of Egypt, who was in charge. And it was safer to trust Him than to put their confidence in any military alliance.

For us the message could not have been clearer. Our natural inclination would have been to take up the offer of a free flight to safety. But what could be safer than to be where God had put us? We prayed through the passage. The challenge was a call to faith, not flight. We were there because we believed God had put us there to do a job. His promise was that He would be with us. We identified with our Javanese brothers and sisters in Christ. We were to stay put. Trust. The outcome, whatever it turned out to be, was in His hands. We felt it right to let it rest there. So what happened next?

With what we felt to be an encouragement to trust the Lord no matter how bad things appeared to be, we each went back to our several ministries working with the local church and the Christian University. Things became increasingly tense for us. But that was also true for our Javanese brothers and sisters. It was right that we stayed with them. The communist propaganda directed to us as foreigners was decidedly unpleasant. The fears faced by the church no less frightening. The economy had been devastated by years of hyperinflation. In areas to the south of where we were working people were starving to death. They were tough times.

In the event for us personally, Adèle's hospitalisation and diagnosis of tuberculosis meant that we had to leave some months after that Bible study for a spell of medical treatment in Scotland. Most of our missionary colleagues stayed on in their ministry.

Not that long after we had left for the UK, the PKI – Partai Komunis Indonesia – finally launched its bloody coup. They started off their attempt dramatically. Killing off the leading generals of the armed forces they threw their bodies into a disused well.[1] One general, Soeharto (later to become President) was spared, and it was under his leadership that the armed forces were to suppress the coup. They showed no mercy. The communist party and its adherents were simply butchered.

The coup suppressed, there followed a time of merciless wholesale massacre as anti-Communist zealots hunted down any who had supported the coup. The recriminations were savage in the extreme – the bloodbath became a time for settling old scores – the unpleasant situation Adèle and I encountered as we returned to ministry after her time of convalescence in Braemar.

By the grace of God, in all the upheavals and horrendous vendettas of those days not one of our mission team

---

1. Peristiwa Lubang Buaya – (Crocodile Pit) On 1 October 1965, PKI members from Lubang Buaya set out to kidnap seven army generals. They returned with the bodies of three generals who had been killed in the kidnap attempt with another four prisoners who they killed. All seven bodies were dumped down a disused well.

suffered physical injury . We had put our trust in the Lord for whatever the eventual outcome might be. It was not an easy decision but in His goodness and mercy the Lord had kept all of us from any serious harm from hostile political factions. He had His own way of dealing with those forces and factors beyond our understanding at that moment of decision and certainly beyond our control. He proved to be the one who was in control. He proved to be 'our refuge and strength, an ever-present help in trouble' (Ps. 46:1).

As we faced the very tangible dangers we thought we could see some parallels with the early church when it found itself in danger from aggressive political forces. Persecution had broken out. Peter and John had been hauled before the Sanhedrin. They had been released but were warned not to preach again in the name of Jesus. An order they had no intention of obeying.

They, of course, did not have the temptation of offers from the British Royal Air Force. There were no Hercules aircraft to ferry them to safety when the storm of persecution broke out in Jerusalem. Being human, they must have been tempted to run, but they didn't. Instinctively they knew where to turn.

They prayed their situation into the second Psalm. Here they discovered a key to their situation. It helped them to overcome their fearfulness. Despite appearances to the contrary, they were assured that God had not been taken by surprise. Everything was firmly in His control. Luke records:

> On their release, Peter and John went back to their own people and reported all that the chief priests and elders had said to them. When they heard this, they raised their voices together in prayer to God. 'Sovereign Lord,' they said, 'you made the heaven and the earth and the sea, and everything in them. You spoke by the Holy Spirit through the mouth of your servant, our father David:

Why do the nations rage, and the peoples plot in vain? The kings of the earth take their stand and the rulers gather together against the Lord and against his Anointed One.'

Indeed, Herod and Pontius Pilate met together with the Gentiles and the people of Israel in this city to conspire against your holy servant Jesus, whom you anointed. They did what your power and will had decided beforehand should happen. Now, Lord, consider their threats and enable your servants to speak your word with great boldness. Stretch out your hand to heal and perform miraculous signs and wonders through the name of your holy servant Jesus (Acts 4:23-30).

Peter's fearless statement to the Sanhedrin that he had healed the man in the name of Jesus Christ of Nazareth 'whom you crucified' had done little to endear him to them. They could have had Peter crucified there and then, and he knew it. Yet, fearlessly he went on to say to them: 'Salvation is found in no one else, for there is no other name under heaven given to men by which we must be saved' (Acts 4:12). His head was fair and square on the chopping block. But what this Psalm taught the young church was that it was God, not the kings and rulers or any members of the Sanhedrin, who was controlling the situation.

'Now faith is being sure of what we hope for and certain of what we do not see' (Heb. 11:1). Their faith was evident in that they saw what others could not see. Soaked, as they were, in God's Word, they knew, despite all appearances to the contrary, that their God was the 'Sovereign Lord.' That governed their reaction in the hour of crisis and gave them confident assurance. They were in safe hands.

Even the cross, which at the time had seemed to be an unspeakable tragedy, was something God had planned from all eternity. For He was 'the Lamb that was slain from the creation of the world' (Rev. 13:8). As Peter had said at Pentecost: 'This man was handed over to you by God's set purpose and foreknowledge; and you, with the help of wicked men, put him to death by nailing him to the cross' (Acts 2:23). That truth now reassured them as they prayed on: 'they did what your power and will had decided beforehand should happen.' It was not that God sanctioned the evil done to His Son, but in His sovereignty even the deeds of those evil men had been taken into account in the outworking of His purposes for redemption. The most criminal miscarriage of justice of all time, clear evidence of the rebellion of kings and rulers, would not have the last word.

By faith they could see beyond the world of time and space. That was more important than anything they were experiencing at that moment in Jerusalem. What they saw by faith was that the Psalm went beyond any historical incident. Here was truth with a universal and eternal significance. God is establishing His kingdom on earth. The fact that the world stands in rebellion against that kingdom was known before time began. We need to grasp that perspective today.

It is not our politicians and presidents who control the destiny of our world, but our Sovereign Lord. He has His own agenda and is moving everything inexorably towards that day when as Habakkuk reminds us: 'The earth will be filled with the knowledge of the glory of the Lord, as the waters cover the sea' (Hab. 2:14).

That message runs through Scripture to the very last book, Revelation. There the curtains are drawn back to show us a throne at the heart of the universe. God is on that throne. He rules, and that rule encompasses even the chaos we see in the nations around us today. The truth is, as expressed by another of the Psalms: 'The Lord reigns, let the nations tremble; he sits enthroned between the cherubim, let the earth shake. Great is the Lord in Zion; he is exalted over all the nations' (Rev. 99:1-2).

Chapters four and five of Revelation describe that throne. For John, incarcerated for his faith on the barren rock of an island called Patmos, that vision was meant to be an encouragement. But John sees a problem. Something is wrong. There is a scroll in God's hand. But for reasons John cannot understand, it remains sealed. It seems that no one is qualified or able to open the scroll or to look inside. That brings tears to John's eyes. Is the occupant of the throne unable to rule and does that mean John is left at the mercy of evil powers?

The tears vanish as he hears that 'the Lion of the tribe of Judah, the Root of David, has triumphed. He is able to open the scroll and its seven seals' (Rev. 5:5). He looks up expecting to see a lion, but instead he sees 'a Lamb, looking as if it had been slain, standing in the centre of the throne' (Rev. 5:6). And he knows, better than anyone, that this lamb bearing the marks of His slaughter is none other than Jesus, the Anointed One, his Lord and Saviour. The one who after His resurrection had said to him: 'All authority in heaven and on earth has been given to me. Therefore, go and make disciples of all nations' (Matt. 28:18-19).

John sees who is shaping history; the one who is in charge, even of his suffering in prison. It is the Lord and His Anointed One who will bring everything to that great climax when all the nations will bow, and every tongue will confess Jesus Christ to be Lord (See Phil. 2:8-11).

The throne governs the universe. Everything must be seen from that viewpoint. Nothing is excluded from God's rule. And when all hell seems to break loose around us, we may feel fearful, but it is God, not the devil nor the powers of evil abroad in the world, that we are to fear.

The devil would want us to fear him. He is delighted if we think of him in equal terms with God. The scale of his deception is enormous. He is out to get us to attribute to him God-like powers that he does not possess. He is, after all, 'the father of lies' (John 8:44).

Thanks to Star Wars, many of us view the devil as if he were 'the dark side of the force' – God's opposite. That is exactly the blasphemous claim Satan wants us to believe. God has no opposites. God is unique. As C. S. Lewis said in the preface to his *Screwtape Letters*:

> The commonest question is whether I really 'believe in the Devil'. Now, if by 'the Devil' you mean a power opposite to God and, like God, self-existent from all eternity, the answer is certainly No. There is no uncreated being except God. God has no opposite. No being could attain a 'perfect badness' opposite to the perfect goodness of God; for when you have taken away every kind of good thing (intelligence, will, memory, energy, and existence itself) there would be none of him left.

> The proper question is whether I believe in devils. I do. That is to say, I believe in angels, and I believe that some of these, by the abuse of their free will, have become enemies to God and, as a corollary, to us. These we may call devils. They do not differ in nature from good angels, but their nature is depraved. Devil is the opposite of angel only as Bad Man is the opposite of Good Man. Satan, as the leader or dictator of devils, is the opposite, not of God, but of Michael.[2]

Satan is a formidable enemy. We must never underestimate him. But it is the fear of God that is the beginning of wisdom and knowledge, (Prov. 1:7; 9:10) not a preoccupation with the devil and the powers of evil.

2. Lewis, C. S., *The Screwtape Letters* (New York City, NY: Harper Collins, 2012).

That truth Jesus emphasised when He said that we were not to 'be afraid of those who kill the body and after that can do no more' (Luke 12:4). Rather He told us in the strongest possible terms who it is we are to fear: 'I will show you whom you should fear: Fear him who after the killing of the body has power to throw you into hell. Yes, I tell you, fear him' (Luke 12:5).

And to underline that same truth, Jesus called Himself 'the stone the builders rejected' (Luke 20:17) and gave us this warning: 'Everyone who falls on that stone will be broken to pieces, but he on whom it falls will be crushed' (Luke 20:18).

Only a reverence, respect and sense of awe for God can bring us the quiet assurance of His love and sovereignty with all the uncertainties that surround us in today's world.

He is still on the throne; we continue to pray, 'Your Kingdom come (Matt. 6:10). Your will be done.' We commit our way to him (Phil. 4:6-7); we trust, obey and leave the outcome in His hands, confident of the promise that being both the Good Shepherd as well as our Sovereign Lord, He will never leave us, we are safe eternally, even when called to face walking through the valley of the shadow of death (See Ps. 23:4; John 10:11, 27-30).

CHAPTER 8

Making Sense of our Troubled World

Why do the nations rage? – Psalm 2:1

What made the Apostles turn to the second Psalm for help when the Sanhedrin was out for their blood? The answer surely is that those scriptures that spoke of God as their Sovereign Lord were the assurance they needed that their destiny was in His hands alone.

As a child I remember seeing vast wall charts covered with strange looking beasts all over them, an artist's impression of the visions from the book of Revelation. The charts, so we were to understand, spelt out in detail God's plan for the end-times. Master the chart and you knew exactly what to expect – more or less. Those who preached from their charts seemed to be pulling rabbits out of hats – something that should have put me on my guard. As a boy of ten I was overawed.

As the years have gone by, I have not been able to find these specific 'rabbits' in Scripture. What I do see is that Jesus will one day return to this world in great triumph. He will bring everything to a glorious consummation. Before that climactic event he warned us that there would be 'wars and rumours of wars' in 'the last days' – that time between His first and second coming – and warned us about being ready for Him when He does come. All that is crystal clear.

With 24/7 news coverage we have more than just 'rumours of wars' – the wars are played out before our eyes. With the escalation of violence and global terror ever more apparent there seem to be parallels with the cyclic intensification of evil and destruction portrayed by the visions in the book of Revelation. The heightened significance of climate change and the plagues predicted for the last times would all seem to be further indicators, perhaps, that our Lord's return might not be long delayed. Certainly, here are many warnings that should alert us to making sure we are ready for our Lord's return whenever that event, in the power and wisdom of God the Father, should eventually take place.

What the second Psalm gives us is an overarching perspective on what is going on in our world. 'Now pay attention … here comes the technical bit.' We will need to read through the Psalm.

It may make things clearer, as we read, to think of it as starting off with a prologue by a Commentator or chorus, as Shakespeare would have called it. Today it would be the role of the TV commentator or a political affairs editor. The chorus introduces us to world governments and politicians, and their reaction to any suggestion that they ought to submit to God's rule and authority. The Commentator then comments on their actions and reactions.

After that, the scene shifts from earth and we eavesdrop on a dialogue between the Lord God and His Anointed One. This has been stimulated by the politicians' rebellious attitude to God's rule and authority. We may have firsthand evidence on our TV screens as to what world leaders at the United Nations are saying in the Security Council but here in this Psalm we glimpse the unseen council in heaven. There we learn of the authority the Lord God has given to His Anointed One – His Son. And after being privy to that scene, our reporter returns to challenge us with the implications this has for us in our world.

Psalm Two

The Commentator
The issue of a global rebellion
Why do the nations conspire ('rage')
and the peoples plot in vain?
The kings of the earth take their stand
and the rulers gather together
against the LORD
and against his Anointed One.

The conspiracy of world rulers
'Let us break their chains,' they say,
'and throw off their fetters.'

God's Response
God's assessment of their rebellion
The One enthroned in heaven laughs;
the Lord scoffs at them.
Then he rebukes them in his anger
and terrifies them in his wrath, saying,

God's action
'I have installed my King
on Zion, my holy hill

God's commission
I will proclaim the decree of the LORD:

He said to me, 'You are my Son;
today I have become your Father.

God's promise

Ask of me,
and I will make the nations your inheritance,
the ends of the earth your possession.
You will rule them with an iron scepter;
you will dash them to pieces like pottery.
'

The Commentator
The warning and appeal to all rebels

Therefore, you kings, be wise;
be warned, you rulers of the earth.
Serve the LORD with fear
and rejoice with trembling.
Kiss the Son, lest he be angry
and you be destroyed in your way,
for his wrath can flare up in a moment.
Blessed are all who take refuge in him.

Now it could help our understanding to know where this Psalm came from. Clearly it is connected with some historical event of considerable significance – a royal coronation at a time of rebellion. But just whose coronation was it? And what rebellion is it talking about?

The simple answer to both questions is: we simply don't know. Perhaps, if we did, we might feel it was limited to that event alone. However, the way in which the New Testament writers return again and again to this Psalm indicates that to them it had an application that went beyond any specific event.

According to the apostles (see Acts 4:25), David wrote this Psalm. Clearly, it moves on beyond David and through the royal dynasty of the house of David – a Psalm fitting for the coronation of all Israel and Judah's kings. Its underlying premise applies to all wise rulers: submission to God, the ultimate authority and ruler of all.

The imagery of war and rebellion may have come from David's firsthand experience. But clearly from the way the Jews, along with New Testament writers, viewed the Psalm, it pointed directly to great David's greater Son – the coming Messiah.

The six-pointed Star of David on Israel's flag serves as a reminder of the great significance of the Davidic dynasty. The origins of that star are shrouded in mystery, but it has become the most common and universally recognised sign of Jewish identity and embodies their messianic hope. That 'hope' is based on the golden age when David was the greatest warrior-king Israel had ever known. The kings who followed David were a disappointment. Only the Messiah-King would fulfil all that the Psalm foretold. The final destiny to which the Psalm points is the final victory of the Lord God and His Messiah – and that is the clear message that heaven takes up in the book of Revelation when it sings: 'The kingdom of the world has become the kingdom of our Lord and of his Christ, and he will reign for ever and ever' (Rev. 11:15).

The king referred to in the Psalm is called 'the Lord's Anointed One.' That word 'anointed' is the word 'Messiah' in the Hebrew or 'Christ' in the Greek. The psalmist shows us how the 'Lord's Anointed One' is appointed as God's Viceroy on earth. As Lord of the Earth, He is the one to whom the nations are to give their allegiance.

In one sense every king of Israel anointed by a prophet was an 'anointed one' – 'a messiah.' If he was a true 'Defender of the Faith' of Israel and lived in submission to God, then his rule carried divine authority. As God's chosen servant and representative on earth he would enjoy God's protection and authority in the execution of his office. The fact of history, however, was that most of Israel's kings failed miserably on all counts. They did not live up to the ideal.

It is only in Jesus that the Psalm finds fulfilment. Israel and Judah's royal families were, for the most part, a disgrace. Understandably, their subjects lost respect for them as they failed in their duties as leaders.

The dialogue behind the Psalm is significant. It is between the Lord God and His Anointed One. As the Psalm unfolds it alternates between this world of time and space to the timeless counsels of eternity. Another way to understand it is to think of it as having four sections:

1. THE WORLD ABOUT US vv. 1-3

We begin the Psalm with a look around us.

First voice – the Commentator

He starts where we are – on earth and facing troubles. He looks at the state of the world about him much as we have been doing in these preceding chapters and he cries out – 'Why do the nations rage?' (Ps. 2:1).

Second voice – The Politicians

Part of the answer to his question comes as he listens in on the counsels and deliberations of world leaders. They brazenly declare their independence from the Almighty and, specifically, want to break from any ties that would bind them to God and His Anointed One. 'Let us free ourselves from their rule,' they say; 'let us throw off their control' (Ps. 2:3 TEV).

2. THE GOD ABOVE US vv. 4-6

The scene then shifts to a secret dialogue that starts in heaven – the principal characters being the Lord and His Son, the Messiah.

Speaker – The Lord God

The Lord God is first to speak. He laughs derisively over the futility of the 'politicians' rebellion and all their efforts to run affairs of state without Him. His laughter is not amusement. It is a sense of incredulity that politicians and presidents should think they could succeed in running His world without any intention of submitting to Him as its Creator.

But it is no laughing matter – it makes Him angry. And in righteous anger He declares that despite the rulers' desire to go it alone, He installs His King Messiah on Zion, His holy hill. And while this world takes steps to put an end to the rule of His Christ, God treats that with the derision it deserves.

3. THE GOD AMONG US vv. 7-9

With mention of Zion we return once again to earth – for the God above us is Immanuel – the God among us. It is then that we hear the Son speaking.

Speaker – the Son

He refers to 'the decree of the Lord.' In that decree God has instructed Him to ask to be given the nations and ends of the earth as an inheritance and the authority to rule over them with a rod of iron.

That rule of Christ is seen as a *fait accompli* by heaven, but it is something that has still to be worked out on earth. And it is to the New Testament that we turn to see how it is accomplished. From there we learn that Jesus began this rule when He rose from the dead and ascended to heaven to sit down at the right hand of God,[1] 'from whence he will come to judge the living and the dead.'

4. THE MISSION BEFORE US vv. 10-12

Now our commentator brings us the challenge. He brings us down to earth with a bump. The application of all that has been revealed is to be taken seriously as we face our world.

Speaker – The Commentator

Then comes an appeal to the powers that be – the kings, rulers, politicians, presidents, and governments – that they be wise. They will never thwart God's ultimate purpose to install His Messiah King. They will never ultimately prevent His rule from extending over all the earth. Those who come under His rule will find Him to be a source of blessing and a refuge. Those who resist will find nothing but will be left to face His wrath – and discover that 'it is a dreadful thing to fall into the hands of the living God.' (Heb. 10:31)

Their only hope is to bow before the Lord God and His Christ and offer their loyalty. Failure to comply will bring wrath. It is only faith and trust in Christ that will bring refuge and happiness (10-12).

A clearer mandate for world mission could not be found anywhere. For all authority from the Lord God has been given to the Lord's 'Anointed One.'

As we listen to our Lord's last words to His disciples, we find echoes of this Psalm when He says:

---

1. Matthew 28:18; Ephesians 1:20-22; 1 Peter 3:22; Revelation 1:5; 2:26-27.

> All authority in heaven and on earth has been given to me. Therefore go and make disciples of all nations, baptising them in the name of the Father and of the Son and of the Holy Spirit, and teaching them to obey everything I have commanded you. And surely I am with you always, to the very end of the age (Matt. 28:18).

Here in this Psalm we are given a broad perspective on our world of time from a viewpoint that is timeless. A glimpse behind the scenes. Clearly the Psalm does not end with a mushy multi-faith appeal for us to go into the entire world and preach comfortable spirituality. It is the uniqueness of the Anointed One, Christ, that comes through loud and clear – the unequivocal message that all men and women everywhere must submit to Him or experience God's wrath.

The clear point at issue here is that apart from Christ we have nothing to offer this world. He is the unique revelation of God to our world. 'In the past God spoke to our forefathers through the prophets at many times and in various ways, but in these last days he has spoken to us by his Son' (Heb. 1:1-2).

Fear may drive us to make compromising statements about what we believe. Of course, all people everywhere have a right to choose what they wish to believe. But that freedom of choice in no way compromises our conviction that salvation is to be found in Christ alone (See Matt. 28:18 TEV). The Bible is never vague on that issue.

Vagueness is the current vogue when it comes to matters of faith. But such vagueness cannot alter God's truth. Writing to his congregation in Glasgow Dr. Sinclair Ferguson said:

> To speak of Him as God incarnate, the only Saviour, as humanity's only hope in modern pluralistic Britain, is no

longer socially tolerated and certainly not politically correct. Orthodox Christian witness now stands condemned by the worst of all pejorative modern terms: 'fundamentalism.'

We have been called to be Christ's witnesses in this society. Most of us daily experience that same pressure to dumb down Christian witness in the office or hospital, in our places of recreation, in the neighbourhood and perhaps even in the family. It is not easy to be Christ's in modern Britain …

A positive way to look at it is this: we are called to serve Christ today in a context just like that of the first Christians – one in which Jesus was tolerated so long as no one made exclusive claims for Him; okay to say 'Jesus is *my* Lord; not okay to say 'Jesus is *the* Lord.'

CHAPTER 9

The Truth Underlying History

The state of our world today is one of organized insanity –
Dr Martyn Lloyd Jones

The gentle, pink warmth of the cherry blossom-lined avenues along the waterfront was in stark contrast to the harsh reality of everything that was going on in the UN building behind us. It was a maze of corridors, offices and conference rooms where solemn dignitaries walked purposefully about their business. Politicians and diplomats in dark suits stood huddled in earnest discussion, relieved by the occasional splash of bright colour – an African delegate in national dress. Hustle and bustle on every side. And, weaving our way through it all, we walked, crocodile fashion, like an expectant group of school children following their teacher.

Our 'teacher', Natasha, hardly fit the stereotype. She was stylishly petite and smart, a young woman from Belarus who looked for all the world as if she had just sprung from the parallel bars of some Olympic gymnasium. Dressed in an impeccable two-piece suit, she spoke perfect English with the merest trace of an accent to betray her roots. Her grasp of all that was going on was impressive. She was politically astute.

As we approached the first conference room our way was barred.

'They're in session. Can't go in. Major decisions. Shaping history!' Her solemn tone was conspiratorial.

And there was something sobering about the fact that all that separated us from the 'major decisions' that were 'shaping history' was the thickness of a wooden door. A small group of men and women locked in conference, grappling with issues that affected the fate of thousands. It called for reflection.

Just a few minutes before, we had been in a different world, the mayhem that is Grand Central Station. Entertained, we had watched the crowds rushing madly about their business through New York's sculptured art deco marble cathedral. We waited and watched to see whether any of the Hollywood Greats would appear. They didn't – or if they did, we missed them. Cary Grant running to board his train to Chicago was conspicuous by his absence. So, not too surprised, we set off down 42nd Street to the eastern waterfront. A few hundred yards, and the rush of the city was forgotten. We were inside the United Nations complex. An island – a secular 'Vatican' – in the heart of 'the World's Capital.'

But it wasn't just the cherry blossoms outside that clashed with the reality within. It was what our guide did not say that made me think. Living and working with the Javanese for over twenty years taught me to listen for what is not said. The Javanese, in their refined politeness, have developed subtlety into an art form. To grasp what they may really be saying you have to learn the art of sifting their words. It is important to discover what has been left unsaid. Often it was silence on an issue that spoke volumes. Natasha did not beat about the bush in her commentary on the UN. She did not consciously omit anything as far as we could see. But I was reacting to what she had left unsaid. Did she really believe that it was the deliberations of the people in this building that shaped history?

For me that was a statement too far. Today's events become tomorrow's history. But far from shaping our history, more often than not history has an unfathomable dynamic of its own. Presidents and politicians grapple with issues on a global scale, but the deep crosscurrents of competing human value systems ultimately defy any human ability to direct, let alone control, the outcome. Listening to some of the debates that take place in the UN, it is hard not to feel that forces are at work that are beyond our human ability to control. No wonder the Psalmist asks, 'Why do the nations rage?'

The phrase is evocative of violent mobs of angry rioters rampaging in mass demonstrations. One commentator paraphrases the verse as: 'Why is the great tumult of nations mustering for war?' Much of our news coverage on TV shows us more of this kind of thing than we care to watch. World superpowers marshalling their troops for war, rioting anarchist mobs venting their anger, anti-globalisation demonstrators wantonly destroying property, wild fund-amentalist extremists shooting off their Kalashnikovs into the air.

The word indicating the uproar in the first verse is rendered differently in various translations. That is because the word means more than just uproar. It carries a sinister implication captured by the translators of the NIV to indicate that it is not a mere storm in a teacup. The rage is evidence of a disturbing conspiracy – 'Why do the nations conspire, and the peoples plot in vain?' (Ps. 2:1).

To 'conspire'[1] is to do something against the law. An unlawful action agreed in secret – a scheme to cooperate towards a common end. And that is what the nations are pictured as doing in their angry conspiracy against God. Such a 'conspiracy theory' behind all the turmoil we see in the nations raises questions. What is it about? And who is behind it all?

The question finds immediate answer in the text. The conspiracy is all about rejecting the rule and authority of God. And specifically here it is portrayed as involving those who represent us – our kings and rulers.

'The kings of the earth take their stand and the rulers gather together against the LORD and against his Anointed One. "Let us break their chains," they say, "and throw off their fetters"' (Ps. 2:2-3), as if they were sitting like some UN council deliberating on world issues and, in particular, the right of the Lord and His Christ to rule over them.

The nations: 'the peoples and nations, as if in a tumultuous assembly, raging with a fury like the raging of the sea, designing to resist God's government'[2] is how the Jamieson, Fausset and Brown Bible Commentary paraphrases the verse. Matthew Henry in his commentary writes: 'They rage and fret; they gnash their teeth for vexation at the setting up of Christ's kingdom; it creates in them the utmost uneasiness and fills them with indignation.'[3] In other words,

---

1. The Hebrew word *ragash* signifies uproar, turmoil and rage – the preferred choice of some translations – but *ragash* is rage with a dark side – conspiracy ...

2. Jamieson, Fausset and Brown; "Commentary on the Whole Bible"; Oliphants:1961; p. 407.

3. Henry, Matthew, *Matthew Henry's Commentary – on Psalm 2* (London: Mashall, Morgan and Scott, 1960), p. 579.

the conspiracy has a focus. That focus is the rule of God. The conspiracy is therefore a concerted opposition to the establishment of Christ's kingdom on earth.

And that of course anticipates an answer as to who is behind it. Basically, the struggle is between heaven and hell. Satan is 'the prince of the power of the very air we breathe in and the god of the world we live in' (Matthew Henry) and his kingdom is well established. When the kingdom of God gains, he loses. Martin Luther's well-known hymn reassures us that: 'His doom is writ; a word shall quickly slay him.'[4] But that does not mean that he is about to give up without a struggle of cosmic proportions.

When Jesus came into our world, 'a second Adam to the fight and to the rescue came.' And His coming was a declaration of war. The powers of evil went into high gear and the evidence for that is found throughout the Gospels. The words with which Jesus opened His ministry, 'Repent for the kingdom of heaven is near' (Matt. 4:17), threw down the gauntlet to those powers of evil. And when He taught His followers to pray, 'Your kingdom come, your will be done, on earth as it is in heaven' (Matt. 6:10), He was teaching us a principle of life that would inevitably mean a confrontation with a world that has joined the silent conspiracy and says, 'Let us free ourselves from their rule, … let us throw off their control' (Psalm 2:3 GNT).

From its opening verse we see how New Testament writers viewed this Psalm as a key to understanding the world around them. It took them to the core issue. One planet with two worlds living side by side. One world praying, 'Our Father in heaven … Your kingdom come, your will be done, on earth as it is in heaven' (Matt. 6:10). The other world turning its back on heaven and saying, 'Let us

---

4. Luther, Martin, 'A Mighty Fortress is our God', c. 1529.

burst their bonds apart and cast away their cords from us' (Ps. 2:3 ESV). In other words – 'freedom – our will be done!'

Diametrically opposite views on the authority of God – this will inevitably mean that those who are serious about following Jesus will be out of step with the world. The world that is united in its stand 'against the LORD and against his Anointed One' (Acts 4:26). This surely is why Jesus warned us that following Him involves a cross. 'In this world you will have trouble' (John 16:33) – we'd better believe it!

I watched with admiration on one occasion as our British foreign secretary delivered a speech at the United Nations in New York one day, only to fly back home across the Atlantic to escort some of the UN officials around the corridors of 10 Downing Street the very next day. One wonders at the dedication of these men and women burning themselves out as they jet-set between the world's capitals in their never-ending round of diplomatic endeavour to find the answer to the question, 'Why do the nations rage?'

What this second Psalm shows us, however, is that they, like all of us, are involved, whether consciously or not, in this silent conspiracy. We live in a world that rejects the rule and authority of God. Tragically that is not something they are likely to factor into their deliberations at the UN! They, like the vast majority of all those whom they represent, do not treat the Maker's handbook seriously.

Some things our governments legislate for fly in the face of God's Word. It begins with two fundamental truths from the very first chapter of the Bible being rejected; the first: 'In the beginning God created … '; and the second simply: 'God created Man in his own image … male and female he created them' (Gen. 1:1, 27). From issues surrounding abortion, environmental pollution, climate change, gender identity, to the tragic indifference shown in addressing the appalling situations that exist in the poorer world countries. These are the tip of the iceberg against which the Titanic of our once Christian culture is now foundering.

Of course, we recognise that many decent men and women are honourable, serious, and work earnestly for those things that are right and just within the parameters of their ideological framework. It is righteousness that exalts a nation but when God's revelation of righteousness is ignored, we and they are in a parlous state.

We live in a 'three-minute culture.' Thanks to the media and our seeming inability to concentrate for more than a few minutes, few people have the patience to sit and listen to reasoned arguments. We live on sound bites. But as the song by Don Schlitz and Paul Overstreet puts it:

> Try as I may I could never explain what I hear when you don't say a thing … You say it best when you say nothing at all.[5]

And it is the sound bites we never hear from our leaders that give the clue. Silence on issues where God speaks. Evidence of complicity in the silent conspiracy that says: 'Let us break their chains … and throw off their fetters.' 'Let us free ourselves from their rule … let us throw off their control.'

The sum of their combined wisdom is to ignore God. Far from that being a passive omission, it is an aggressive opposition to the kingdom of God and all those who seek to live in the 'obedience that comes from faith' (Rom. 1:5). They fail to recognise their recklessness in ignoring those guidelines that God has set out for us in His Word for our own good.

---

5. Overstreet, Paul, and Schlitz, Don, 'When you say nothing at all', 1988.

The 'chains and fetters' referred to in the Psalm are words taken from the world of agriculture – the bridle, bit and reins. All of them designed for the control and well-being of the animal and its rider. Seen in that light their conspiracy to break their chains and throw off their fetters is the height of madness.

When driving through the rice fields along potholed roads in Java, it was not unusual to come suddenly upon a slow lumbering cart being drawn by a couple of weary-looking water buffaloes. On a good day, these carts probably reach a maximum speed of around two miles an hour. From time to time you would find one parked at the roadside, its driver scooping water from a nearby ditch to throw over the beasts to cool them down. They, poor animals, lived for the time when they could be unhitched and led off into some muddy pool for a final cool off at the end of the day. Such an ox-cart lumbering in your path as you rounded a corner at speed could be unnerving.

But just as long as the driver wasn't asleep, and the yoke and reins were in place, all was well. The animals would continue on a predictably straight course. No peasant in his right mind would dream of taking his unwieldy cart onto the highway without the yoke and reins firmly in place. With the shimmering heat haze rising from the tarmac and cars screaming past at speeds only a fatalist would attempt, it was the one thing that ensured safety for all concerned. Only a madman would throw away the reins.

While I was still in high school, I spent Saturday mornings earning pocket money as a 'grease monkey' servicing cars. I developed a lifelong love for cars. As an engineering student I built my first homemade sports car based on a 1928 Austin Seven chassis. A great deal of time had been spent modifying the old beam axle at the front. It was cut in half and converted into a simple form of swing axle independent suspension. That was relatively easy. The difficult part came in trying to modify the steering linkage. That took time and effort. The connection between the steering wheel and road needed to be more than just wishful thinking! What kind of foolish engineer would I have been if I had said, 'the new suspension is so smooth – I won't bother about the brakes and steering'? No mechanic worth his salt would say, 'Let's ignore the steering, throw away the track rods and forget the ball joints.' But that is the level of mankind's foolish rebellion against God.

As a Mission Director in the UK, one of our more pleasant tasks was the opportunity to visit with our missionaries in East Asia. On one visit to Sapporo in the Island of Hokkaido, Japan, Adele and I were sent off to the south on our own. We were going to visit Chefoo, Nanae – one of our schools for the missionaries' children. Not knowing a word of Japanese, and being totally mystified by the Japanese script, we were concerned to know where to get off the train.

'Oh, you just get off at nineteen minutes past four,' Irene Hope informed us.

'But supposing the train is late?' we asked.

'It won't be – unless there's an earthquake,' came her confident reply.

Before we could find out what we should do if there was an earthquake, the train had set off down the platform. At 4:19 p.m. precisely we drew into our station and were met by a reception committee of excited children. This was Japan. We would never dare to predict its arrival so accurately here in the UK.

Ask any British Rail commuter and you will get a very different story. We don't need anything as outlandish as an earthquake to make our trains late. Leaves on the line, powdered snow, vandalism, and failure of the driver to show up, track repairs, fog … our rail services can come up with the most bizarre list of excuses. They may work hard to try and overcome the problems and improve the service. But as far as I know no one has yet suggested: 'Let's tear up the tracks and throw away the signals.'

Yet here, in a nutshell, is the madness of our twenty-first century rebellion. We have thrown away those guiding rails the Creator has laid down for us in His handbook. With one thousand cubic centimetres of grey matter and a few neurons between our ears we dare to believe that we can run our lives and our world without reference to the Creator. We have exchanged the law of God for license. If it seems right or feels good, then go for it. Everyone does what is right in his or her own eyes. Is it any wonder there is so much fear and uncertainty?

What with communist uprisings and the upheavals around election times we have had more experiences of riots in Java than we care to think about. When anarchistic mobs rampaged through the streets of Jakarta, reason was abandoned. It was blind chaos. Mayhem. The rule of law meant nothing. Shops were looted and burned. Cars were overturned. People were shot, clubbed, knifed, killed. It was terrifying to have to experience.

When mobs run amuck, law and order break down. Panic reaches fever pitch. Reason is thrown to the winds. The law of the jungle takes over. And then suddenly, as if someone has pulled a switch the mobs slowly melt away into the back streets and an eerie calm takes over. Apart from an odd individual picking his way through the debris, the streets are empty. The atmosphere is electric. You look nervously in all directions. You feel naked and vulnerable.

It is not until you see, through the smoking wreckage littered across the road, the forces of law and order in their armoured cars, that a sense of security is restored. Troops station themselves at intervals on either side of the road. Slowly normality returns and the tension eases. People reappear and walk down to what is left of the shops. Little by little life returns to normal. And you realise that the bit and bridle supplied by the law, far from being a straitjacket, is a life jacket. Just so, God's Word was not given to destroy liberty but to make us truly free. Jesus said, 'I am come that they might have life, and that they might have it more abundantly' (John 10:10 KJV).

Frequently we watch statesmen log countless hours in their attempts to solve world crises. The frightening awareness of the destructive power of evil drives all of us to seek solutions. Yet tragically the cycle of violence is not broken. We watch nations and world movements set against one another and any who do not feel a sense of dismay and fear are, in Mrs Beaver's words, either 'braver than most or else just silly.' The clear evidence of what happens when a world tries to live without God is all about us.

Shortly before he passed away Dr Martyn Lloyd Jones preached from this second Psalm at a gathering in Glasgow. He spoke of the international tensions of the time and, while evil has been with us from the beginning of history, his statement then that 'the state of our world today is one of organised insanity' seems totally relevant today.

The Psalmist's opening 'why?' may not have been a question so much as an expression of incredulity. How can we be so foolish as to think that we can live as God intended us to live without reference to the guidelines He laid down for us in His Word? To live without God is to live 'imagining a vain thing.' The silent conspiracy of our world will not succeed. God will have His way. The wonder is that for that to come about He so loved this rebellious world that He sent His only Son that all who will accept Him to be their Lord, will discover His saving love and mercy. And the Psalm indicates there is still more to be said about that.

CHAPTER 10

The Meeting of Wrath and Mercy

... a guilty world is washed by love's pure stream. –
Graham Kendrick

As we read on into the next section of the Second Psalm, we find something that on the surface seems disturbing. The Psalm looks away from the state of rebellion in the world around us to the God who is enthroned above us. And we find Him laughing. That is worrying.

The fear of the Lord is one thing, but does God mock us in all our troubles? An angry God enthroned who laughs, scoffs, rebukes, terrifies seems to be at variance with all we know of His love and mercy and gracious forgiveness. The passage states:

The One enthroned in heaven laughs; the Lord scoffs at them.
Then he rebukes them in his anger and terrifies them in his wrath, saying,
'I have installed my King on Zion, my holy hill.'
I will proclaim the decree of the Lord:

He said to me, 'You are my Son, today I have become your
Father …' (Ps. 2:4-7).

The section begins by reminding us that when we say that
at the centre of the universe there is a throne, we are not
speaking in physical or geographical terms. God is infinite:

Where can I go from your Spirit?
Where can I flee from your presence?
If I go up to the heavens, you are there;
if I make my bed in the depths, you are there.
If I rise on the wings of the dawn,
if I settle on the far side of the sea,
 even there your hand will guide me,
your right hand will hold me fast (Ps. 139:7-10).

God is without bounds or limits. As Solomon said when he
was dedicating the temple in Jerusalem: 'The heavens, even
the highest heaven, cannot contain you. How much less this
temple I have built!' (1 Kings 8:27).

God has another temple – He dwells in the hearts of the
humble and says to those who mourn for their sins: 'I live in
a high and holy place, but also with him who is contrite and
lowly in spirit' (Isa. 57:15).

However, when the throne of God is specifically mentioned,
it has important significance. It is speaking about God in His
kingly authority (Ps. 11:4; 45:6), and His right to rule the nations
as king of the earth (Ps. 47:7-9); it emphasises His activity as the
righteous judge of us all (Ps. 9:4, 7, 8 cf Rev. 20:11).

So, this Psalm brings us pictures of who God is and some
of the different activities in which He is involved, but for
the Psalmist then to say that coming from the throne is the
sound of laughing (Ps. 2:4-5) is disturbing. The words of
Handel's Messiah ring uncomfortably in our ears – 'the Lord
shall have them in derision.' It goes even further when it

says that God 'rebukes them in his anger and terrifies them in his wrath.'

Obviously, the mocking here is in the context of our rebellion. The unwise enterprise undertaken by those who have conspired against His throne and all it stands for – those who imagine that their rebellion might succeed. Will the kings and rulers of this world usurp His throne? Will mankind do away with God? The thought is absurd – only worthy of contempt and derision, implies the Psalmist. Yet it leaves us asking: How does the Bible's teaching on God's love relate to all this?

God is in no way callous or cruel – He loved us enough to die for us while we were still His enemies (Rom. 5:10). He loved us so much that He sent His only Son into the world that we might have eternal life through faith in Him (John 3:16). So His laughter cannot be the laughter of indifference. The one He sent to this rebellious planet, to save it from the consequences of its rebellion, wept over Jerusalem's refusal to save herself from suffering and destruction (Luke 19:41-44). Therefore we know His heart is not hardened by all the rejection He has experienced. The laughter is rather from a sense of incredulity for all those who, in their arrogance, think they could even run their lives, and this world, without Him. It is the futility of their conspiracy that He mocks. Even to think their rebellion could succeed is ludicrous.

It was in the face of this rebellion that God showed His love. He sent His Son into the world. In our Psalm God says: 'I have installed my King on Zion, my holy hill.' To which the Son replies, 'I will proclaim the decree of the Lord: He said to me, "You are my Son, today I have become your Father."' And so, the God above '... became flesh and made his dwelling among us. ... the One and Only, who came from the Father, full of grace and truth' (John 1:14). 'Immanuel – God with us' (Matt. 1:23).

It was then the earthquake struck as the rebellion gathered momentum – 'He was in the world, and though the world was made through him, the world did not recognise him. He came to that which was his own, but his own did not receive him' (John 1:11). The world took its 'stand … against the LORD and against his Anointed One' (Ps. 2:2).

That was precisely what happened when Pilate presented Jesus to the mobs in Jerusalem. They screamed:

> 'Take him away! Take him away! Crucify him!'
> 'Shall I crucify your king?' Pilate asked.
> 'We have no king but Caesar,' they responded (John 19:15).

The crucifixion appeared to spell defeat. The powers of evil seemed to have triumphed. But at their rebellion, 'The One enthroned in heaven laughs; the Lord scoffs at them' (Ps. 2:4).

The apostles witnessed His resurrection. The cross was not a disaster. In rejecting God's Son, they saw that the authorities only, '… did what your power and will had decided beforehand should happen' (Acts 4:28).

That cross was in the plan of God before the creation of the world (Rev. 13:8). Jesus would rise again from the dead. The rebels were in for a shock. It is here at the cross that all history comes together, for it is both the clearest demonstration to us of God's love and at the same time the severest warning of His wrath, the wrath reflected in those words: 'Then he rebukes them in his anger and terrifies them in his wrath.'

Paul starts his exposition of the gospel of God's grace in Romans by saying that it begins with the revelation of God's wrath directed towards those who suppress the truth about Him (Rom. 1:16-18). God's wrath is a manifestation of His holy, moral character, His repugnance at sin and evil –

burning up and consuming all that corrupts and destroys in His world.

Paul then goes on to explain that this same gospel is the clearest proof we have of God's love. By love he does not mean sentimentality. We live in a world that has so abused the word 'love' as to rob it of its true meaning. The love of God is pure and holy and not incompatible with anger. If God is not a God of wrath, His love is no more than frail, worthless sentimentality. That would mean mercy would be meaningless and the cross nothing but a cruel and unnecessary experience for His Son.

Obviously, there was nothing weak or sentimental about the cross. It stands at the heart of history and is the meeting point of God's wrath and mercy. Everything before the cross points towards it. Everything since the cross looks back to it. It is God's answer to the heart of the world's problem.

Here we face deep mystery. Titanic forces in an unbearable tension. The omnipotent, righteous, all-loving Creator rejected by the very people He created. How can He not punish them? We are told that He is a consuming fire (Heb. 12:29). The intensity of that holy fire is so powerful that, were He not Almighty God, He would self-destruct. On the cross it almost seems as if that is what could be happening as Jesus cries out: 'My God, my God, why have you forsaken me?' (Mark 15:34).

Jim Philip, in the Bible study notes he wrote for his congregation, helps us to a deeper understanding of these words: 'My God, my God, why have you forsaken me?' He points out that they take us into the Holy of Holies. It is as if the curtain has been drawn back a fraction and we are allowed a glimpse of the intimate relationship that exists within the Godhead. What we hear the Son saying to His father is stark and alarming. It hints at something unthinkable – disruption in the Godhead. Yet in that mysterious and awful cry from the darkness which hung over the cross, we glimpse the depth of God's holy love for this guilty world.[1]

We tread humbly on holy ground. How could the Lord forsake His Anointed One? How could Christ not understand what was happening if it was all a part of the divine plan from before time began?

Only a few years earlier at His baptism the door of heaven had opened and Jesus had heard the voice from heaven say: 'This is my Son whom I love' (Matt. 3:17). This would have reminded Him of the second Psalm and the fact that He was God's Anointed One. But now after He had just prayed so fervently: 'Father, the hour has come. Glorify your son that your son may glorify you' (John 17:1), there was little evidence of glory in the agony of all He was passing through. Only abandonment. Little prospect, from a human perspective, of fulfilling the messianic hope the Psalm had promised.

Crucifixion ranks with the most sadistic, barbaric and savage deaths ever devised by mankind. Through the centuries artists have magnified its horror. But art can never portray the real horror of what was happening when Jesus hung on the cross. It may even be guilty of doing the opposite. Art, by getting us to focus our attention on the physical and external, may cause us to overlook the truly awesome nature of that event.

This was no mere martyrdom. Many martyrs have faced death courageously. If Jesus' death were only a martyr's death, then it would have been tragic but not remarkable. What Jesus faced was something far more terrible than martyrdom. He faced what no one has yet faced – 'the

---

1. Philip, James; From the Daily reading notes from James Philip – Holyrood Abbey Church on Matthew 27:46. See: http://www.thetron.org/resources/the-james-philip-archives/bible-readings/ Last accessed February 2020.

second death.'[2] That death which is the 'wages of sin' (Rom. 6:23). That is what the writer to the Hebrews means when he says that Jesus by the grace of God 'suffered death … so that … he might taste death for everyone' (Heb. 2:9). That is why His total identification with our humanity was so important:

> Since the children have flesh and blood, he too shared in their humanity so that by his death he might destroy him who holds the power of death—that is, the devil—and free those who all their lives were held in slavery by their fear of death. (Heb. 2:14-15)

For Him to identify with us completely He had to identify with the punishment we deserve.

The Apostles' Creed captures the unthinkable when it says: 'He descended into hell.' Hell, not to be thought of here in terms of physical geography but in its essence – abandonment by God – that abyss which is the consequence of sin – 'the second death.'

Yet the more we think about it, the deeper the mystery becomes. How could the sinless Son of God, one with the Father and the Holy Spirit from all eternity, be separated from the Father? How could He not know why?

In his great passage on the reconciling love of God in Christ, Paul writes, 'God made him who had no sin to be sin for us, so that in him we might become the righteousness of God' (2 Cor. 5:21).

Those six words – 'He was made sin for us' – take us to the heart of His suffering on the cross. Sin cuts us off from God. The sinless Son of God was made sin. He stood before God as the most wicked of all people.

---

2. Revelation 2:11; 20:6, 14; 21:8.

He was taking on Himself all that our rebellion meant and facing the consequences. God was exposing Him to the wrath and anger that our sin merits. For Jesus to 'be the firstborn among many brothers' (Rom. 8:29) and bring 'many sons to glory' (Heb. 2:10) that was what was involved; He was made to be our sin. He became all that we are, all that is rotten, and all that is shameful in us.

Is it any wonder that Isaiah, speaking of the suffering servant, said that those who looked at Him were: 'Appalled … his appearance was so disfigured beyond that of any man and his form marred beyond human likeness' (Isa. 52:14).

The one who was from eternity 'the radiance of God's glory and the exact representation of his being' (Heb. 1:3), on the cross was made sin and became so disfigured and marred that He was no longer recognisable as truly human. As Alec Motyer has said in his commentary on this verse from Isaiah, such was the revulsion 'that those who saw him stepped back in horror, not only saying, "Is this the Servant?" but "Is this human?"'[3]

It is on the cross that I see the horror of my sin. It is hard to express this, but that disfigured object of horror Jesus became on the cross was a reflection of me and all the gross distortion of my sin. All the horror of what I am in my rebellion, exposed to the wrath of God in His Son. Christ suffers the judgement that is properly mine. The wrath that is revealed 'against all the godlessness and wickedness of men who suppress the truth by their wickedness' (Rom. 1:18) is at the same time the clearest expression of His holy love by which we are reconciled to Him. As someone has said, 'On the cross God saw me at my worst, and on the cross God loved me most.'

---

3. Motyer, Alec, *The Prophesy of Isaiah* (London: IVP, 1993), p. 425.

And yet Jesus cries out 'Why?' The question is, why did He ask why? He had gone to the cross willingly. He had said that He laid down His life for the sheep, no one took it from Him, but He lay it down willingly (John 10:17-18). He knew from the beginning of His mission that to be made sin would involve being abandoned. That was what had appalled Him when He agonised in the garden of Gethsemane and said: 'If it is possible may this cup be taken from me. Yet not as I will, but as you will' (Matt. 26:39). He had known what was coming. Yet from all eternity He had never experienced such a thing. And the horror as He experienced it was the ultimate horror. He descended into hell.

What was it that made Him ask this? The mystery goes deeper. While He had known that being made sin would involve being cut off from the Father, in some sense that we will never be able to understand, He was cut off at that point of time from understanding fully what He was going through. As He hung on the cross, and as for three long hours darkness came over the scene, He was not only separated from His Father, but even separated from understanding fully what He was going through.

If Jesus had gone through it all, conscious that everything would turn out all right in the end, His identification with us would have been compromised. Instead He plumbed the depths of the horror of sin.

As James Philip summed it up in his church's study notes:

> It was there, at that point, where the Son of God lost the last, final consciousness of the Father's love – there, that atonement was made, and pardon bought and won for us.[4]

4. Philip, James; From the Daily reading notes from James Philip. See: http://www.thetron.org/resources/the-james-philip-archives/bible-readings/ Last accessed February 2020.

Anne Cousins' expression of these deep truths in her hymn can hardly be bettered:

> Jehovah lifted up his rod,
> O Christ, it fell on thee!
> Thou wast sore stricken of thy God;
> There's not one stroke for me.
> Thy tears, thy blood, beneath it flowed;
> Thy bruising healeth me.
>
> Death and the curse were in our cup –
> O Christ, 'twas full for thee;
> But thou hast drained the last dark drop -
> 'tis empty now for me
> That bitter cup -- love drank it up;
> Now blessings draught for me.[5]

What then will Jehovah, the Lord of Heaven and Earth, do with those who despise His grace, spurn His mercy and reject the atonement His Son made for us on the cross? And what is going to happen to all those who, in ignoring His authority, persist in their silent conspiracy?

The Apostle John gives us an indication of the answer to that question when he writes: 'Whoever believes in the Son has eternal life, but whoever rejects the Son will not see life, for God's wrath remains on him' (John 3:36). And the cross shows us just what God's wrath can do. For in judging sin He did not spare even His own Son.

The cross stands in the world of time, at the heart of history, and it shows us that without God exercising wrath against sin, His love would be no more than frail, worthless sentimentality, and the whole concept of His mercy would have no meaning.

---

5. Cousins, Anne Ross, 'O Christ, what burdens bowed thy head', (1824-1906).

So, in the light of the cross, Scripture asks: 'How shall we escape if we ignore such a great salvation?' (Heb. 2:3). The simple answer is: there is no escape! The only hope for our world lies in embracing this salvation.

The world's rebellion is doomed to fail. There is no way it can succeed. We face a missionary confrontation with those who are in rebellion. Only through repentance and faith in Him will they discover the salvation that will bring them to the liberty of 'the obedience that comes from faith' (Rom 1:5).

As the missiologist Herbert J. Kane has written:

> God prefers salvation to judgement. Herein lies the missionary element. God's wrath makes the gospel necessary: his love makes it possible.[6]

The words of Kendrick's beautiful hymn seem the only appropriate response we can make:

We worship at your feet
Where wrath and mercy meet
And a guilty world is washed by love's pure stream
For us he was made sin
Oh, help me take it in
Deep wounds of love cry out 'Father, forgive'
I worship, I worship the lamb that was slain.[7]

6. Kane, J. Herbert, *Christian Missions in Biblical Perspective* (Grand Rapids, MI: Baker BookHouse, 1979), p. 20.

7. Graham Kendrick , 'Come and See (We worship at your feet)' - copyright – Make Way Music, Used by permission.

CHAPTER 11

The Kiss of Life

Your kingdom come; your will be done on earth, as it is in heaven. – Matthew 6:10

If Jesus is the Lord of all and if a day is coming when every knee will bow before Him, and if He has commanded us to make disciples of all nations, then the logic is not hard to follow. We face a missionary challenge – to take the message of the uniqueness of Christ and His lordship to all men and women everywhere.

The second Psalm reminds us that mission did not suddenly appear on the pages of the New Testament. It was in the heart of God from the dawn of time. The mandate for mission is found in the very first verse of Scripture. 'In the beginning God' – it is God's world. He made it. We are His creation. He has the sovereign right to our allegiance. And as God Almighty, He will have that obedience.

The message of the second Psalm is simple. Either we bow in worship and accept His love and mercy, or we will be forced one day to face the terror of His wrath.

Our missionary appeal is summed up in the closing warning of the Psalm:

> Therefore, you kings, be wise; be warned, you rulers of the earth. Serve the LORD with fear and rejoice with trembling. Kiss the Son, lest he be angry, and you be destroyed in your way, for his wrath can flare up in a moment. Blessed are all who take refuge in him (Ps. 2:10-12).

One day everyone will bow to the Son of God. There will be no choice in the matter. He will judge the nations (Matt. 25:31-32). For all those who have accepted His mercy it will be joy; for those who have persisted in their rebellion, terror. That applies at a personal level, but it has significance for the whole of society.

The Bible is full of exciting promises assuring us of God's love, His mercy, His saving grace and His faithfulness. And as believers we are encouraged to claim those promises and delight in them all. However, there are other promises; promises that warn of the consequences of persisting in rebellion. These are equally valid. They speak of God's wrath. They warn against making a shipwreck of our lives. Truths that as disciples of Christ we dare not soft-pedal simply because our society, in the conspiracy of its rebellion, has decided to label them as 'politically incorrect.'

One statement from the writer to the Hebrews is a reminder that those who continue in rebellion will discover a side of God they would rather not know. 'For ... it is a dreadful thing to fall into the hands of the living God' (Heb. 10:30-31). We are to alert men and women to that aspect of God's promises.

The last book of the Bible tells us that at the end of time a day is coming when heaven will cry out:

> The kingdom of the world has become the kingdom of our Lord and of his Christ, and he will reign for ever and ever (Rev. 11:15).

It goes on to give thanks to God that He has established His reign in power in the words of the second Psalm:

> The nations were angry; and your wrath has come. The time has come for judging the dead (Rev. 11:15-18).

The rage and rebellion against Christ is doomed from the start. It is futile. It cannot possibly succeed (Rev. 19:19-21). And at the end of time the awesome wrath of Almighty God will deal with the feeble fury of the kings and rulers of this world and all who have said, 'Let us break their chains ... and throw off their fetters' (Ps. 2:3).

The Scriptures paint a graphic and frightening picture of God's wrath – a truly awesome picture of what that will mean for all who continue in their silent conspiracy:

> Then the kings of the earth, the princes, the generals, the rich, the mighty, and every slave and every free man hid in caves and among the rocks of the mountains. They called to the mountains and the rocks, 'Fall on us and hide us from the face of him who sits on the throne and from the wrath of the Lamb! For the great day of their wrath has come, and who can stand?' (Rev. 6:15-17).

It is not popular to speak of God getting angry. It is not comfortable, and it is not an easy thing to do. But the Psalm warns that 'his wrath can flare up in a moment' and that is a message we must take seriously as we fulfil Jesus' great commission. Not in any spirit of belligerence, but with that winsomeness and concern that reflects the love that God demonstrated at Calvary. A holy love so intolerant of sin that it has borne the full consequences of its own intolerance.

At the cross God's wrath and mercy met. By the cross two destinies become clear. The one accepts His mercy. The other chooses to face His wrath. The one will kiss the

Son and can say: 'Since we have now been justified by his blood, how much more shall we be saved from God's wrath through him!' (Rom. 5:9). The other on that final day will echo those awesome words 'My God, my God, why have you forsaken *me*?' Words which will be lost forever in that place of meaningless and abandonment which is hell.

The world may be hostile. But a realisation of the fate of those who persist in their rebellion adds urgency to our obedience to the great commission. 'We are therefore Christ's ambassadors' (2 Cor. 5:20) and every one of us who submits to Him as Lord is sent by Him to implore men and women to be reconciled to God. It is in the awareness of having been commissioned with the message of reconciliation that we are to urge men and women 'not to receive God's grace in vain' (2 Cor. 6:1).

We are sent to be salt and light to a world in rebellion. We are sent to establish another kingdom – not a kingdom of this world, but a kingdom where Christ as the Lord rules and directs the hearts of men and women who will bow to Him.

And when we pray: 'Your kingdom come, your will be done on earth as it is in heaven' (Matt. 6:10), we pray a missionary prayer, and in so doing we put our own service and ministry on the line, to be at God's disposal. We cannot ignore what this prayer means in the context of what the second Psalm is saying. The coming of His kingdom, while it is a blessing for His people, is anything but a blessing for those who have not kissed the Son and bowed to His authority. This warning must be taken seriously. It needs to be sounded above a diluted version of the gospel that places its emphasis on health, wealth and happiness. Why so? 'For his wrath can flare up in a moment.'

If we look at the very first Psalm in the Psalter, we will see it speaks of two humanities existing side by side in our world, the one evil and the other good. The one in rebellion, the other in submission. The one saying, 'My will be done, my kingdom come.' The other delighting in God's Word and praying, 'Your kingdom come, your will be done on earth, as it is in heaven.'

And those two humanities face two destinies. As C.S. Lewis says in *The Great Divorce*:

> There are only two kinds of people in the end: those who say to God, 'Thy will be done,' and those to whom God says, in the end, 'Thy will be done.' All that are in Hell choose it. Without that self-choice there could be no Hell. No soul that seriously and constantly desires joy will ever miss it. Those who seek find. Those who knock it is opened.[1]

The Bible speaks of two families. One, it calls the family of Adam, the other the family of Christ. By birth we are sons and daughters of Adam. That is our natural family – in rebellion and oriented towards going its own way without reference to God. It is from that family that we inherit a nature that will lie and cheat, if we think we can get away with it. It is characterised by a personality that lives for itself. The side of us that responds instinctively to the 'Go on, spoil yourself' or the 'If it feels good, do it' messages fed to us by the media.

This self-centred family of the Old Adam is what we are born into and it is committed to the silent conspiracy. Our mission, as followers of Christ, is to call men and women to join the family of the New Adam – Christ's family. A family we can only enter by being born again by the Spirit of God. A family of those who seek to live for God and His kingdom.

---

1. Lewis, C. S., *The Great Divorce* (New York City, NY: Harper Collins, 1977), pp. 66-67.

> And he died for all, that those who live should no longer live for themselves but for him who died for them and was raised again. (2 Cor. 5:15)

This is what the death of Christ for us was all about. A denial of all that being 'in Adam' means. An embracing of all that being 'in Christ' brings as God in Christ shares the life of His humanity with us. That is where we discover the radical answer to the world's rebellion. We are called to go into all the world and make disciples.

After the particular manifestation of evil at Dunblane, the Rev Eric Alexander wrote:

> Our … response must be to tremble at the frightening potential of evil in the world and (don't forget) in our own hearts too. We live in a society which takes evil lightly, regards it as a plaything, frowns on those who want to curb its freedom, and gorges itself (worse, allows its children to gorge themselves) on televised, videoed, filmed or live portrayals of the worst excesses of human depravity. Indeed, our society idolizes those who represent that. And then we are surprised that we have produced the likes of Thomas Hamilton. What a callous insult to Dunblane's sorrows it would be, if our national boldness and carelessness about evil remained unaffected …

He went on to say that we must show:

> … a new confidence in the gospel of Jesus Christ with its life-changing power, and a new desire to commend the only Saviour of sinners, in ever more winsome ways to a sick, violent and godless world, Nothing but the radical transforming power of Jesus Christ can bring hope to such a world.[2]

2. Alexander, E. J., The Bulletin – Minister's letter to his Congregation of St George's Tron Glasgow, March 1996.

This transforming power of Jesus, the gospel, is no mere smearing of ointment on the forehead but the destruction of the old in order to start the new. By His death and resurrection that break with the old becomes possible. 'If anyone is in Christ, he is a new creation; the old has gone, the new has come!' (2 Cor. 5:17).

Hence, we are to take the message that all men and women everywhere are to kiss the Son, lest he be angry. Subjects of the king showed homage and allegiance to their king by kissing his hand. To kiss here speaks of worship and submission (cf. 1 Kings 19:18; Hosea 13:2). So the call is for worship and submission to Christ's lordship and authority.

The appeal, while it applies to everyone, is clearly addressed very pointedly to leaders and governments. They bear a special responsibility in office for the example they set. As Calvin says in his *Institutes*, world leaders are not to 'lay aside their authority and return to private life, but to make the power with which they are invested subject to Christ, that he may rule over all.'[3] Wise leaders will exercise their authority and leadership, leading lives of submission, not rebellion, to God and His revealed Word. That is the only antidote to the arrogance of power evident in many leaders as they strut the world stage. The same principle applies to them in their leadership of the nations they represent for 'the fear of the Lord is the beginning of wisdom, and knowledge of the Holy One is understanding.' (Prov. 9:10).

Sadly, today when we hear God's name invoked it is little more that the first utterance of some verbally challenged individual expressing surprise. Tragically the sacred name has been reduced to the level of an exclamation mark. The

---

3. Calvin, John; 'The Institutes Of The Christian Religion'; Book IV; Wm.B. Eerdmans;1989; p. 654.

fear of God has been lost and with it the wisdom that comes from above. There is no lack of knowledge, but knowledge divorced from the fear of the Lord is a dangerous thing.

It is said that we get the leaders we deserve. When our leaders show a loss of respect for their Christian heritage, they are only reflecting the changed culture from which now they have come. We should not be surprised if the breakdown of law and order in our society increases. By comprehensively ignoring God's Word, we have lit the fuse for our nation's implosion. Our ultimate problem in the Western world is not terrorism. Our ultimate problem is that we have failed to submit to the authority of God.

'Righteousness exalts a nation, but sin is a disgrace to any people' (Prov. 14:34). History has many terrible stories to tell us that theme. The out and out anti-God super-rogues stand as warning beacons – Genghis Kahn, Herod, Hitler, Stalin, Pol Pot, Mao Tse-tung, Osama bin Laden, along with the Saddam Hussein's of this world who are prepared to gas and slaughter their own people. Their arrogance and greed have brought untold suffering to millions. Any leader who fails to see how crucial it is to acknowledge the sovereignty of God and recognise the responsibility of stewardship they hold in their position of leadership is open to the danger of pride.

As a child, whenever I heard the Creed recited, I thought they were saying that Jesus 'suffered under Pompous Pilate.' When we read John's account of Jesus standing before the governor, we realise that 'pompous' fits this man perfectly. Here is this puny man standing before the one who not only made him in the first place, but who had flung the stars into space. Here he stands, face to face with the one who is his 'sovereign Lord' (whether he likes the thought or not) and he has the temerity to say to Him: 'Don't you realise that I have power either to free you or to crucify you?'

There is something ludicrous in the scenario. The one who made the heavens and the earth; who with but a thought could have blown this man away, the one who controls the destiny of planet earth, Immanuel, God with us, stands meekly before this pompous little man and lets him continue. What meekness there is in His quiet reply: 'You would have no power over me if it were not given to you from above' (John 19:11).

Did the earth tremble as He spoke, I wonder?

Pilate had got it wrong. As have so many of his modern successors. As the humbler of them will freely confess, politicians do not have the power they would like or imagine they have. Ultimately, God alone directs world history. He is the one to raise up and put down world powers even though they may fail to realise what is going on behind the scenes.

To say that is not to impugn the commitment and goodwill of so many of our leaders. Many are good and sincere men and women of integrity. And we know that by the common grace of God they are granted a measure of success, and we enjoy a measure of peace under their leadership. We are encouraged to pray for that (1 Tim. 2:1-4). But if they fail to acknowledge their limitations and fail to recognise that there is a God in heaven, they court the danger that goes with an unwarranted sense of self-importance.

The prime example of that kind of pride going before a fall is in Daniel's story of Nebuchadnezzar. When that man, in the land today called Iraq, looked over his kingdom, he is reported as saying: 'Is not this the great Babylon I have built as the royal residence, by my mighty power and for the glory of my majesty?' (Dan. 4:30). God in His mercy didn't let him get away with his conceit. He was driven out to live in a field like an animal for seven years. He only returned to his throne in the palace when, duly humbled, he had finally learned the truth that 'the Most High is sovereign over the kingdoms of men and gives them to anyone he wishes' (Dan. 4:25). Our leaders do well to think hard about that.

In the first sermon he preached after the allied occupation of Stuttgart, Helmut Thielicke described the fall of Germany as Hitler's Third Reich lay in the dust of its own death. Stuttgart was piled high with rubble from the Allied bombing raids, even as he preached. The decimation of Germany's armies on the Eastern Front and the superior strength of her enemies were the external manifestations that finally brought the Nazi regime to its knees. Thielicke saw the deeper truth of what happens when a nation and its leaders lose their fear of God. Despite their Christian heritage, the German people had become unaware of how they had been deceived.

Preaching to them on the Lord's prayer – his sermon is recorded in the book *The Prayer that Spans the World* – he speaks of:

> The real and most terrible danger: the danger that there is such a thing as the devil who can lead a man about by the nose in the midst of all his idealism, and – that there is a God, upon whom we can wreck ourselves, because he will not be mocked.

He spells out the miscalculations on which their nation was ultimately 'so hideously shipwrecked.' He says, 'It was not the strength of their enemies but, the fact:

- that we did not calculate the factor which is 'God' in our plans and therefore fell victims to megalomania;

- that we violated the commandments of God and therefore got tangled in the towrope of our own unpredictable and brutal instincts;

- that we ignored that monumental call: 'I am the Lord your God, you should have no other gods before me,' and hence were landed in the giddy ecstasy of power-worship which brought the whole world into the field against us;

- that we ceased to trust ourselves to the miracle of God's guidance and therefore put our faith in miracle weapons that never came;

- that we no longer knew that God is in heaven and man is on earth and therefore could not help but lose all sense of the real proportions of life and consequently were also stricken with blindness in the purely external spheres of political and military relationships.'[4]

Behind the visible 'the invisible is mightier and more creative and destructive in history than the visible.' He continues:

Anybody who still has not grasped that our nation ... was wrecked precisely on this dangerous rock called 'God' and nothing else has no eyes to see. He no longer sees the forest for the trees, and because he sees only individual catastrophes, he no longer sees the basic, cardinal catastrophe which is behind them all.

It is easy to agree that Hitler, Pol Pot and Mao Tse Tung all deserve to burn in Hell. But the warning is for all of us: 'there

---

4. Thielke, Helmut, *The Prayer That Spans The World – Sermons on the Lord's Prayer*; translated from the German (Cambridge: James Clarke & Co, 1965), pp. 117-119.

is a God, upon whom we can wreck ourselves, because He will not be mocked.' Ultimately for each of these men it was God who was their downfall. They were wrecked on God. They stand before us as warnings.

It may not be in fashion to assume the dogma of racial superiority to which Hitler held. The West, however, could still be deceiving itself by a false trust placed in its moral superiority as it wages its War against Terror. Forget the one who has said 'I am the Lord your God, you shall have no other gods before me,' and the real proportions of life may be lost.

Hegel, the German philosopher, is often quoted as saying: 'History teaches us that history teaches us nothing!' What it ought to teach us is that our real enemy may not be who we think it is. The West stands in danger of being deceived by the arrogance of power. The arrogance that destroyed the Nazi regime. Thielicke's warning comes from the bitter ashes of that misplaced trust.

> We can never put too much trust in Jesus, and we can never put too little trust in ourselves.[5]

---

5. Ibid.

CHAPTER 12

The Death of Death

… all flesh shall see his glory.

There was a very definite 'kerrlunk' – (something my spell checker does not recognise) – but the sound of terminal finality from the front axle was more than recognisable. Sitting three to a hard seat and sharing the jarring ride over the potholed road with goats, chickens and even a pig in a basket, it was almost a relief, initially, to be ordered out to the freedom of the roadside. The sense of liberty did not last, however. The driver and his assistant disappeared beneath the front end of the bus and after a few feeble tapping noises, appeared to relax quietly in the shade and fall asleep. There was certainly little evidence of any more progress on the engineering front. For the rest of us it was Ramadan, midday and blazing hot. The trees being conspicuous by their absence; it all added up to no shade, no drinks, no food and no transport. The heat I could feel burning through my shirt and reflecting upwards from the yellow dusty earth. Even my trusty black Clarks shoes had turned pale yellow.

We waited and sweated. We had come from Makassar and were not far from the Buginese town of Pare-Pare, halfway to the Toraja Highlands. It was the point at which the main road gave way to an unmade track. When another vehicle, optimistically calling itself a bus, finally hove into sight and offered to transport us to Pare-Pare, we all got in or on depending on our agility. I think those on top of the luggage on top of the bus probably had the pleasantest ride, but we were grateful to be moving again and ended up spending the night in the home of a good Muslim family in Pare-Pare.

At around three o'clock in the morning I was kindly wakened by my host and invited to share in *suhur*, the rich breakfast feast eaten before dawn to set up the faithful for the day of fasting ahead of them. The women of the household had been up all night cooking and I had hardly slept for all the noise and chatter. There in the room was an immense smorgasbord and as the honoured, if unexpected, guest I was given the seat of honour and plied with plate after plate of delicacies. I remember a Muslim friend of ours complaining one year that she did not have enough money to fast. If this is what the fasting ritual involved, it was hardly surprising. Just as so many of us overspend on Christmas food and feasting, so it appeared this family made sure that their fast was preceded by a feast. You certainly needed a few hours respite before you felt like eating again.

I was heading north to visit some of our missionaries working in Toraja. Many Indonesians who live in the green valleys of Toraja had become Christians. Some cynics suggested they had turned to Christianity so they could eat pork and drink tuak – fermented palm wine. Clearly many of them had little grasp on what it meant to follow Christ. There was a never-ending tug of war with indigenous animist beliefs. The root issue was: who is Lord? Christ or the ancestors? It is a society trapped in a social web of death. Death is the cornerstone of their culture. And these death rituals are the number one tourist attraction of the region

– the income supplementing their lifestyle and easing the cost burden of their funerals.

The onward journey over unmade roads from Pare-Pare to Makale seemed to take forever. Another breakdown fixed this time with lashings of rattan and bamboo, and after several weary miles of dry tracks winding round the hillsides, we found ourselves entering a beautiful new world. Craggy mountains, palm trees, bamboo and lush banana trees surrounding villages of traditional Torajanese houses set in an emerald sea of paddy fields. And, blessed relief, it was several degrees cooler. We stood at the entrance to a large secluded valley surrounded by hills and mountains, a landscape of limestone formations, terraced valleys and wooded hills with something of the Shangri-La about it. But like Shangri-La, not everything is as it seems. This is the land where the dead rule the living, and the living find themselves overwhelmed by the demands made on them by the dead.

Sunday found me preaching at one of the local churches and after the service an elder came into the vestry and wept. I had been speaking of Jesus as the bread of life but, as for so many others in Toraja, it was death, not life that was his problem.

It is said of the Torajanese that they live to die. In Britain funerals generally take place within a few days of death. In Torajanese terms it takes a long time to 'die.' Death has become a mix of rituals, custom, social life and spectacle. The dead are regarded as being as much a part of society as the living. So, across the rice fields where they work you can see cliffs rising precipitously with balconies carved high into the solid rock face. These balconies are crypts. They house the mortal remains of Toraja nobility. And standing propped up in the balconies is a row of macabre wooden dolls representing the deceased. The effigies are dressed in a sarong and their sightless eyes look out impassively over the rice fields where the dead had once worked. Once a year their effigies are taken down, washed, reclothed and replaced back in their balconies.

Lower down the cliffs, a network of coffin-filled caves reaches deep into the limestone caves. As you walk inside skeletons tumbling out of wooden coffins greet you. Skulls sit side by side on rock ledges. Bones and old coffins lie open in gruesome disarray. Since the souls of their ancestors are residing in a spirit world elsewhere busily ensuring the fertility of the rice fields, it is seemingly appropriate that their earthly remains should be on display for us. Little food offerings lie here and there just in case any of them need to 'eat.' The birds look fat.

The reason for it all is that the spirits of the ancestors have to be kept happy. After all, they are thought to wield a vast amount of power over daily life. They are seen as the lords of the earth. It is they who confer good crops, health, and fertility on their descendants. So, if you dishonour or displease an ancestor at their funeral ceremony you could be in serious trouble. Crops could fail. Wives and daughters could be subject to miscarriages. Accidents could happen. Others could die.

Which brings us back to our elder in the vestry. He had experienced two tragic deaths in his family. They had been given a Christian funeral. He had refused to go through with the customary death rituals. Then one of his children had died. And suddenly he came under immense pressure from his family. They accused him of actually causing the child's death by refusing to perform the correct rites for the other members of the family. He was a man at his wits' end. So, he had given in, and gone through with the ceremonies, but then had come to realise that what he had done was a denial of his faith. He was desperate. He needed to confess his lack of faith and find the Lord's forgiveness.

It is hard for us to realise what such a culture of death is like. It is woven into the warp and woof of this society. Distant family members will come back home from all over the islands of Indonesia for a family funeral. Matters of inheritance are somehow determined by how much each of the children contributes to the ceremony. The 'accounting' procedures as to who gets what, by way of what, are known as 'meat debts'; these are incredibly complex and worked out according to rules handed down through the centuries. Some of the village elders have memorised who owes what and to whom. The social order is built on this web of death and surviving family members vie for position and influence as they try to outdo one another. The rich flaunt their status. The poor feel despair. And for Christians, breaking the cycle of such a culture can make them into social outcasts.

When someone is 'ready' to have a funeral, whole villages from the surrounding valleys will arrive in a procession at the home of the deceased. Temporary houses will be built for the guests. They will stay for around a week or so, all at the expense of the grieving family. The family therefore can become burdened with debts that take many years to pay off. Feasts, chants, rituals, cockfights and buffalo fights all must be laid on for the guests.

And central to it all is the killing of buffalo. Buffaloes are a symbol of wealth; and for the deceased to reach heaven and be well supplied, they need buffalo sacrifices. The animals, especially the expensive white buffaloes, are important and sacred. The status of a family and the success of the funeral are determined by the number of buffalo sacrificed. Around fifteen would be a normal number but sometimes as many as a hundred may be killed if the deceased was rich or of noble birth.

Because the cost and planning are such a drain on resources, the event may not take place for months or even years after someone has died. There are two stages. Until the funeral, the body is treated with chemicals and kept in the family's house. During this period the dead relative is described as 'sick'. After all, they are far safer kept in the house rather than being allowed to meddle around in the spirit world until they have been given a proper send-off or their spirits might just come back and blight your crops. To keep up the illusion and reassure the deceased that they are only 'sick' until they have had their funeral, they are offered food each day.

As the journalist Jenifer Hile wrote in a National Geographic Magazine article, 'the smell of gradual decay is accepted as part of life in Toraja.' The tragedy is that with all the turmoil of our world, the 'smell of gradual decay' is part of life for all of us. In the words of the old hymn: 'Death and decay in all around I see ... '

But it is precisely here in the resurrection of the Lord's Anointed One that we discover the secret of God's victory over our rebellion. On the Day of Pentecost, Peter said: 'God raised him (Jesus) from the dead, freeing him from the agony of death, because it was impossible for death to keep its hold on him' (Acts 2:24). He quoted from the sixteenth Psalm, 'nor will you let your Holy One see decay' (Acts 2:27). indicating that David foresaw the resurrection of the Messiah and His victory over death and decay. The same theme recurs elsewhere in the New Testament where Paul reminds us that while death and decay is what we now see in the world, a day of glory is coming when 'creation itself will be liberated from its bondage to decay ... ' (Rom. 8:21).

In the heat of the tropics the decay and smell of death is inescapable. This is why normally funerals take place straight away. The Torajanese are an exception. As if to counteract the smell of decay, mourners in some parts of Java will throw Eau de Cologne, flowers or spices into the open coffin. But nothing can hide the grim reality, the horror, the finality of death. In more affluent societies with the help of refrigerators and air-conditioned mortuaries, death has been sanitised. People are not so conscious of the cruel reality of decay. Death is somewhat of a taboo subject – it is rarely talked about. Yet it is the one fact of life none of us can ultimately ignore. And while we may push thoughts of death out of our minds, when someone we know dies or is killed, it is then the fear buried deep in our minds will surface. And who, if we are honest, is not fearful? Death is so final – or is it?

Jesus came to break us out of the web of fear which death can bring. It was said of Him that He identified with us in becoming human so that 'through death he might destroy him that had the power of death, that is, the devil; and deliver them who through fear of death were all their lifetime subject to bondage' (Heb. 2:14-15 kjv). Yet as He was taken down from the cross it looked as if death had won.

Those to whom He came were united in their hatred of God's Anointed One and said: 'Here is the son, come let us kill him … we will not have this man to reign over us.' [1]They crucified Him. They rolled a stone over His grave and sealed it. And they congratulated themselves on the success of their rebellion. But – 'the One enthroned in heaven laughs; the Lord scoffs at them.'

Those soldiers commissioned to guard His tomb had the most futile job imaginable. It was pointless. There was something ironic in their trying to lock the Creator of heaven and earth in a cave. No wonder the Lord has them in derision. 'Vainly they seal the dead.' He is the Lord of life – He is the Resurrection and the Life.

---

1. Cf Mark 12:1-12 , with John 19:15.

Once again C. S. Lewis in *The Lion, the Witch and the Wardrobe* has given us a beautiful picture. The witch at the stone table has slaughtered the great lion Aslan. He had offered his life to save the traitor, Edmund, whom the witch had captured. As Aslan dies, it appears that the wicked witch has triumphed. An atmosphere of black despair is everywhere. Aslan's two companions, Susan and Lucy, are numb with grief. They wait and watch while Aslan lies dead on the stone table. Then, feeling cold, the two of them go for a short walk. Suddenly, as their backs are turned, they hear a deafening crack. The stone table has broken in two, and to their shock Aslan has disappeared.

But their horror and despair turn to joy when Aslan suddenly reappears. They can scarcely believe what they are seeing. As Lewis tells the story:

> 'What does this all mean?' asked Susan … 'It means,' says Aslan, 'that though the Witch knew the deep magic, there is a magic deeper still which she did not know. Her knowledge goes back only to the dawn of time. But if she could have looked a little further back, into the stillness and the darkness before Time dawned, she would have read a different incantation. She would have known that when a willing victim, who had committed no treachery was killed in a traitor's stead, the Table would crack and Death itself would start working backwards … '[2]

Death working backwards; death could not hold Him. It merely proved to be the gateway to the proclamation of Christ's kingdom and authority over the nations. For as Paul wrote in Romans, Jesus was 'declared to be the Son of God with power, according to the spirit of holiness, by the resurrection from the dead' (Rom. 1:4 KJV).

---

2. Lewis, C. S., *The Lion the Witch and the Wardrobe* (New York City, NY: Harper Collins, 1980), p. 148.

So, in this Psalm we have the Son saying:

I will proclaim the decree of the LORD: He said to me, 'You are my Son; today I have become your Father. Ask of me, and I will make the nations your inheritance, the ends of the earth your possession. You will rule them with an iron sceptre; you will dash them to pieces like pottery' (Ps. 2:7-9).

And the day of His resurrection becomes the day of His coronation. Which is why, when Paul preached in the synagogue at Pisidian Antioch, he could say:

We tell you the good news: What God promised our fathers he has fulfilled for us, their children, by raising up Jesus. As it is written in the second Psalm:

'You are my Son; today I have become your Father.' ... But the one whom God raised from the dead did not see decay.' (Acts 13:32-37)

Jesus is now ascended to the right hand of God and sitting on the throne 'far above all rule and authority, power and dominion, and every title that can be given, not only in the present age but also in the one to come. And God placed all things under his feet' (Eph. 1:21-22). Jesus was no mere guru or prophet or angel. He was God. He shares the throne of heaven with His Father[3] and all people everywhere will bow to Him as Lord.

In the Psalm He lays claim to His authority over the nations by recounting the 'decree of the Lord' (Ps. 2:7-9). And it was in the full awareness of that decree that He made His 'enthronement speech' before His disciples, telling them that 'all authority in heaven and on earth has been given to me' (Matt. 28:18).

3. Psalm 11:4; 45:6, Revelation. 3:21, Luke 1:32; Acts 2:30 Cf Acts 13:32-37, Hebrews 8:1 Psalm 9:4, 7,8 cf Revelation 20:11, Psalm. 47:7-9.

By announcing to them that the nations were His inheritance and the ends of the earth His possession He was affirming His right. The Lord from heaven is the King of kings and Lord of lords. And on that basis, He issued the Great Commission:

> Therefore, go and make disciples of all nations, baptising them in the name of the Father and of the Son and of the Holy Spirit, and teaching them to obey everything I have commanded you. And surely I am with you always, to the very end of the age. (Matt. 28:18-20)

All Scripture points us forward to that day when echoes from the second Psalm will ring round the courts of heaven: 'The kingdom of the world has become the kingdom of our Lord and of his Christ, and he will reign for ever and ever'. (Rev. 11:15).

The day when Habakkuk's great vision will finally come true and: ' … the earth will be filled with the knowledge of the glory of the LORD, as the waters cover the sea'(Hab. 2:14).

It will also be the day when a new heaven and a new earth will appear. And God will dwell with us and we will live with Him. He will be our God and we will be His people and, on that day, 'He will wipe every tear from their eyes. There will be no more death or mourning or crying or pain, for the old order of things has passed away' (Rev 21:4).

Even Death will die (Rev. 20:14), a truth beautifully expressed in John Donne's sonnet written in the seventeenth century:

> Death be not proud, though some have called thee
> Mighty and dreadful, for thou art not so:
> For those whom thou think'st thou dost overthrow,
> Die not, poor Death, nor yet canst thou kill me;
> From rest and sleep, which but thy pictures be,

Much pleasure, then from thee, much more must flow,
And soonest our best men with thee do go,
Rest of their bones, and souls' delivery!
Thou art slave to fate, chance, kings and desperate men,
And dost with poison, war, and sickness dwell,
And poppy or charms can make us sleep as well,
And better than thy stroke; why swell'st thou then?
One short sleep past, we wake eternally,
And death shall be no more, Death thou shalt die![4]

Of course we cannot begin to imagine what heaven will really be like, but the Bible's language makes it clear that in that day we will at last discover true joy and satisfaction:

> To him who is thirsty I will give to drink without cost from the spring of the water of life. He who overcomes will inherit all this, and I will be his God and he will be my son (Rev. 21:6-7).

All heaven will rejoice and in that day a Hallelujah Chorus will sound such as no choir on earth could ever sing:

> Hallelujah! For our Lord God Almighty reigns.
> Let us rejoice and be glad and give him glory!
> For the wedding of the Lamb has come,
> and his bride has made herself ready (Rev. 19:6-7).

So, the future is bright. The future is glorious. The people of God will enter the fullness of joy that God has prepared. 'Blessed are those who are invited to the wedding supper of the Lamb!' (Rev. 19:9), who go on to live in the city of God where they will discover the light of the glory of God. 'The throne of God and of the Lamb will be in the city, and

---

4. Donne, John, 'Death be not proud', 1609.

His servants will serve Him. They will see His face, and His name will be on their foreheads' (Rev. 22:3-4). Scripture runs out of words in its attempt to describe the glory of the victorious outcome: 'As it is written: "No eye has seen, no ear has heard, no mind has conceived what God has prepared for those who love him"' (1 Cor. 2:9).

On that day, around the throne of God, there will be a great multitude from every nation, tribe, people and language and the subject of their worship will be: 'Salvation belongs to our God, who sits on the throne, and to the Lamb' (Rev. 7:10). And on that day the Lord of the Earth will, as it is so graphically translated in the King James Version, 'He shall see of the travail of his soul, and shall be satisfied' (Isa. 53:11 KJV).

And how is all this going to happen? Our best answer comes through the words of William Fullerton's old hymn:

> I cannot tell how He will win the nations,
> How He will claim His earthly heritage,
> How satisfy the needs and aspirations
> Of East and West, of sinner and of sage.
> But this I know, all flesh shall see His glory,
> And He shall reap the harvest He has sown,
> And some glad day His sun shall shine in splendor
> When He the Saviour, Saviour of the world is known.[5]

What greater contrast could there be to the hopeless bondage and helplessness of the Torajanese culture of death?

---

5. Fullerton, William Young, 'I cannot tell' (1857-1932).

CHAPTER 13

The Fear of Meaninglessness

Providence is a Christian's diary, but not his Bible. – Thomas Watson

There can be few more numbing experiences than having to work on an assembly line in a car factory. Keeping pace with a moving belt, condemned to repeat the same operation over and over again. I know. I've tried it. While studying engineering as a Student Apprentice by courtesy of the Ford Motor Company, some of us had the unique experience when our college had its summer vacation of being allowed to do practical studies in production engineering methods in the factory at Dagenham.

On one occasion during my vacation from engineering studies at college I asked for, and was granted, permission to work on an assembly line for a week. For forty hours, over five days, I lifted a never-ending succession of flywheel bell housings and put them onto a row of slowly moving gearboxes. With the help of an overhead power tool that I would pull down to each new box, I fastened the bolts holding the two parts together – again and again and again. My back ached; my legs grew tired; my brain died! I have never known time to pass so slowly. The arrival of the tea trolley ladies was a major event. Ten minutes to sit on the floor, my back against a bin full of gearboxes, and a chance to read the newspaper. The half hour lunch break in the canteen was the only ray of sun in the drabness of the day. And when the time came to clock off it would have taken more than a herd of wild horses to stop me from getting to the front of the mob, in the rush to burst through the factory gates to freedom. It was a week when life seemed to have lost all meaning and purpose. I have great sympathy for those millions around the world who earn their bread and butter on a factory assembly line and must pass such a large amount of time with little more purpose to such a large part of their lives.

My original employer is credited with having invented or at least developed the whole concept of mass production around an assembly line. Whether or not it was the sheer monotonous emptiness of life on the assembly line that prompted Henry J. Ford to say that 'History is bunk,' I could not say. Somehow, I doubt whether he spent any of his time tied to the line. But I could be wrong. At least he produced a sound bite that has cheered the heart of many a schoolboy!

What he actually said, however, was more profound and penetrating. The Chicago Tribune in 1916 actually reported him as saying: 'History is more or less bunk. It's tradition. We don't want tradition. We want to live in the present. And the only history that is worth a tinker's damn is the history we make.'

History and the Classics may not have been Henry Ford's strong point. But as an industrialist and a manufacturer of cars he was no fool. He had an objective – to create a car for the masses and make money. To that end he experimented, rationalising different procedures to speed up construction and reduce costs. It was his efforts to achieve his goal that led to the mass production techniques of the assembly line. Model T's rolled off in their millions. His vision was realised. Manufacturing was revolutionised, factory workers dehumanised. He broke the mould. He 'made history'. And at the end of the day it was worth more than a 'tinker's damn' to his shareholders.

History, far from being 'more or less bunk,' has significance. All of us are a part of history. In it we find meaning. The fact that we live means that we 'make history'. It gives us significance and meaning. The wise will discover the particular significance life has for them and the significance they can give to history. To feel that my life has no meaning and that history has no purpose is soul-destroying.

Macbeth's lines on receiving news of his wife's suicide could have come from any factory worker on an assembly line. Only in his case it was the murderous ambition and guilt of Lady Macbeth together with his evil deeds that brought this dark pessimism of meaninglessness:

> To-morrow, and to-morrow, and to-morrow,
> Creeps in this petty pace from day to day
> To the last syllable of recorded time,
> And all our yesterdays have lighted fools
> The way to dusty death.

For him history was not 'more or less bunk' – everything had become meaningless. It had no more meaning other than lighting 'fools the way to dusty death.' There are echoes here from the book of Ecclesiastes, where a life lived without God is so accurately described as, 'utterly meaningless … There is no remembrance of men of old, and even those who are yet to come will not be remembered by those who follow' (Eccl. 1:2,11). He calls life nothing but 'a chasing after the wind.'

With poetic, but deadly, logic Macbeth goes on:

Out, out, brief candle!
Life's but a walking shadow, a poor player
That struts and frets his hour upon the stage
And then is heard no more: it is a tale
Told by an idiot, full of sound and fury, signifying nothing.[1]

A fear that our life has no real meaning or purpose, no more significance than a candle, is not uncommon. If, in fact, I am nothing more than a by-product of some inanimate bang; if I only exist thanks to a random aberration in some primordial soup kitchen, then the reality of the evil I see on all sides brings me nothing but intimations of dread. Am I just a collection of chemicals or at best just an animal with nothing but a form of organic intelligence? Or am I a creature created in God's image made in order to have communion with Him or am I just a chemical aberration? Is there a God? C. S. Lewis poses an elemental problem:

Supposing there was no intelligence behind the universe, no creative mind. In that case, nobody designed my brain for the purpose of thinking. It is merely that when the atoms inside my skull happen, for physical or chemical reasons, to arrange themselves in a certain way, this gives me, as a by-product, the sensation I call thought. But, if so, how can I trust my own thinking to be true? It's like upsetting a milk jug and hoping that the way it splashes itself will give you a map of London. But if I can't trust my own thinking, of course I can't trust the arguments leading to Atheism, and therefore have no reason to be an Atheist, or anything else. Unless I believe in God,

---

1. Shakespeare, William, *Macbeth*, act 5, scene 5.

I cannot believe in thought: so, I can never use thought to disbelieve in God.[2]

If in my worldview there is no place for God, then the logic is frightening. If a righteous, loving God does not exist, what is good and what is evil? Is there any difference or is it all in the mind? And is what I think in my mind only a chain reaction 'when the atoms inside my skull happen, for physical or chemical reasons, to arrange themselves in a certain way?' And if I do sense a fear of evil, where am I to go for protection?

As Sartre put it in his book *Existentialism and Human Emotions*:

Dostoyevsky said, 'If God didn't exist, everything would be possible. … ' Indeed, everything is permissible if God does not exist, and as a result man is forlorn, because neither within him nor without does he find anything to cling to.[3]

Mr Spock, the resolutely logical human-Vulcan first officer of the Star Ship Enterprise of the Star Trek movie, is often quoted as saying; 'There's life, Jim, but not as we know it.' A world without God would bring us logically to the same conclusion. A world without God would be hell.

But we don't live in such a world. This is not hell. God has not removed Himself from His world. Life is not meaningless. We live in time surrounded by the infinity of space and that inescapable sense that there is an ultimate power. As H. G. Wells said with some perception in his unusual book *God the Invisible King*:

---

2. Lewis, C. S., *The Case for Christianity* (Nashville, TN: B&H Publishing, 2000), p. 32.

3. Sartre, Jean-Paul, *Existentialism is a Humanism* (New Haven, CT: Yale University Press; 2007), pp. 28-29.

And those whose acquiescence in the idea of God as merely intellectual are in no better case than those who deny God altogether. They may have all the forms of truth and not divinity. The religion of the atheist with a God-shaped blank at its heart and the persuasion of the unconverted theologian, are both like lamps unlit. The lit lamp has no difference in form from the lamp unlit. But the lit lamp is alive and the lamp unlit is asleep or dead.[4]

That 'God-shaped blank' is in the heart of each of us. Only God can fill the void. Augustine wrote in his 'Confessions':

You stimulate [us] to take pleasure in praising you, because you have made us for yourself, and our hearts are restless until they can find peace in you.[5]

Religion is our human initiative to try and fill that blank space. As Christians we believe it was God, not we ourselves, who took the initiative to fill that blank. It is His nature to communicate. And the God above us became the God among us – Immanuel. John MacArthur has expressed it this way:

All mankind is trapped on planet Earth, captive to time and space and surrounded by an endless universe. Many sense in the deepest parts of their beings that there is an ultimate power or God. And so, they try to discover how they can know this Supreme Being. The result is religion, the invention of man in his attempt to find God.

Christianity, however, teaches that we don't find God, because God has already found us. He has disclosed Himself

4. Wells, H. G., *God the Invisible King*, Kindle version, 2013, Chapter 3.

5. Augustine of Hippo, *The Confessions of St Augustine* (Dover Publications, 2002) p. 1.

to us through His Word. In the Old and New Testaments of Holy Scripture we have the unveiling of God.

The Bible bridges the entire history of the earth. During those long centuries God was always disclosing Himself, because it is in His nature to communicate. An artist paints and a singer sings because the ability is in them. God speaks because He desires to make Himself known to His creatures. Francis Schaeffer, referring to God, wrote, 'He is there, and He is not silent.'

God's revelation of Himself presents us with an understanding of world history from eternity to eternity. It is revolutionary. It tells us that God is not detached from His world. 'In the beginning God created the heavens and the earth' (Gen:1:1). God did not then shoot off to some remote galaxy and hide away. He continues to sustain His creation 'by his powerful word' (Heb. 1:3).

He is the Sovereign Lord (Acts 4:24). History is not more or less bunk; it is something in which God is intimately involved. Under His mighty hand, history has a destiny. It is going somewhere. And since each one of us is a part of developing history, every life has significance and meaning.

Scripture is not in the business of spelling out the specifics of exactly what will happen ten years down the line. Time and space are too vast for one volume to detail all that could happen. Scripture, however, pulls back the curtains to let us see the forces that are at work controlling and shaping the world's destiny. And that is where we must look if we want to find 'a true perspective' when facing the enigma of evil in our world.

What we do discover is that, whatever evil may happen in this world, ultimately God will overrule it for His purposes.

We are to trust Him even when what He allows seems contradictory.

The cross is a supreme example of how God overruled evil for His glory. At times He may make use of strange forces to either protect or correct us as Habakkuk was to learn (Hab. 1:12) and that must deepen our trust in Him even when we do not understand. In the words of F. W. Faber's hymn:

> Thrice blest is he to whom is given
> The instinct that can tell
> That God is on the field when he
> Is most invisible.[6]

Thomas Watson in *A Body of Divinity* expresses it quaintly:

> Indeed as Augustine says well, 'We are beholden to wicked men, who against their wills do us good.' As the corn is beholden to the flail to thresh off its husks, or as the iron is beholden to the file to brighten it, so the godly are beholden to the wicked, though it be against their will, to brighten and refine their graces.[7]

God in His wisdom permits evil – history is proof of that. He allows men and nations to walk in their own ways (Acts 14:16), but that does not mean He has any hand in their evil. He cannot act contrary to His nature. Some things we may not understand. What is clear is that He will ultimately bring good out of it all.

He is the Lord of History. We witness His dealings with nations. Sometimes evil is apparently allowed to flourish unchecked. It even appears to enjoy success. Sometimes

---

6. Faber, Frederick W, 'Workman of God O lose not heart' 1849.

7. Watson, Thomas, A Body of Divinity (Edinburgh: Banner of Truth, 1958), p. 58.

we are tempted to envy the wicked. Like the Psalmists in Psalms 37 and 73 we wonder why it is that some people, who live without any reference to God in their lives, seem to prosper. Psalm 37 encourages us not to let their seeming success undermine our trust in God while Psalm 73 reminds us of their final destiny (Ps. 73:3,16-20). In faith we recognise the providences of God but at the same time we should not equate success as particular proof of God's blessing.

In our personal lives, the words of the Puritan, Thomas Watson, are well worth applying: 'Providence is a Christian's diary, but not his Bible' – an important principle to bear in mind when we testify to the Lord's particular dealings in our lives. As Eric Alexander frequently liked to remind his congregation: 'Christian experience is not the same thing as the experience of some Christians.'

It is in God's Word, not in my experiences, where true meaning is to be found.

The preacher in Ecclesiastes knew the fear of meaninglessness, but finally gives us the answer to a fear of life without meaning when he sums up his 'sermon' with these words: 'Here is the conclusion of the matter: fear God and keep his commandments, for this is the whole duty of man (Eccles. 12:13).

CHAPTER 14

The God of our Future

Blessed are all who take refuge in him. – Psalm 2:12b

It was the rainy season. And it rained as only it can in the tropics. Somehow rain is easier to cope with on holiday when you are on the shores of the Indian Ocean enjoying vast stretches of tropical sand. You get wet from swimming; you get wet from the rain, the sun comes out and you get dry – and it isn't cold. And if you do feel chilled there is all the vast open expanse of a deserted beach with the finest of golden sands on which to play ball, run and jump, turn cartwheels and let off steam. And that is exactly what we did with our four boys.

One day, however, the rains were severe. The coast was being lashed by a cyclone. It was a real struggle to climb up the cliffs to shelter. Our eldest, John, put his small hand in mine. We gripped each other tightly as we struggled against the rain stinging in our faces. For a second we paused for breath. John looked at me, and out came one of those profound theological insights that six-year-olds seem to produce from time to time.

It's all right for him up there, throwing it all down on us here!

And we knew what he meant. Sometimes we feel angry. Often we experience fear of the unknown. A niggling apprehension that God is remote and unconcerned. A worry that He does not realise that I need His help and guidance. A fear that I might not survive forces over which I have no control. Like the Psalmist I look around and ask: 'Why do the nations rage?' And if, like the Psalmist, I realise it is because men and women have rebelled against God, I still ask: then what does the future hold?

As to the shape of the future, none of us can claim to have a hotline to heaven. God has not given us a highly detailed map. And we need to be careful of anyone who claims exclusive visions as to what may or may not come to pass. God's Word does not encourage us to speculate. The emerging paths of history that God has mapped out are His business, not ours (Rom. 11:33-36). What He has told us is in His Word is meant for our trust and obedience. We are not privy to the hidden secrets of His wisdom (Deut. 29:29). He knows it would not always be the kindest thing for us to know the future (Isa. 55:9).

That is not to say, however, that He has not given us guidelines as to how we are to face the future. We have a certain hope and expectation based on His Word (1 Pet. 3:15) and we need to be confident as we tell others of the assurance we have. And while only God knows the details of what will happen in the future, by grace we know the one who is the future. The God of history and Lord of the earth. To know Him is our refuge in troubled times.

As Rene Padilla launched out into full-time service, he said a senior missionary told him: 'God will not give you a map, but he will give you his hand.' There are echoes here of words famously quoted by King George VI as he gave his Christmas message in 1939 when Europe had just been plunged into the horrors of the Second World War:

And I said to the man who stood at the gate of the year:
'Give me a light that I may go safely into the unknown.'
And he replied:
'Go out into the darkness
And put your hand into the hand of God.
That shall be to you better than light
And safer than a known way.'[1]

Of course, it is a perfectly human instinct to want to know what the future holds. Most of us have problems wanting to know what we ought to do next. A young girl talking to me in my vestry one afternoon said: 'If only God would say 'Mary, do this! signed God' I would do it, whatever it was!' Many of us would sympathise. But if we really knew more precisely what was ahead, might we not be tempted to shrink back? After all, we are not given 'dying grace' to live by. But we are given a wonderful promise to keep us from being fearful of what may lie ahead. God says as He had said to Paul dealing with his 'thorn in the flesh' – 'My grace is sufficient for you … ' (2 Cor. 12:9).

We found some of Mary's 'sisters' in one of Tokyo's sophisticated shopping centres. It was a strange sight – a long queue of girls stretching along the pavement, streaming away from the subway entrance. Not going into the subway, as we would have expected, but heading out of the subway onto the road. The line ran in front of a modern department store and ended at a little stall. One by one they disappeared behind the stall to emerge unravelling a small piece of paper – the end of their lunchtime quest. A lucky note from the fortune-teller. Guidance for the future.

In the ancient Akabusa shrine in Tokyo we watched a smart businessman in his mid-twenties shaking a metal canister. A random numbered stick fell to the floor through

---

1. 'The Gate of the Year' – Minnie Louise Haskins (1875-1957).

a small hole in the lid. He took it over to a row of pigeonholes to find a tiny scroll of paper with his word of guidance for the day. What stocks should he buy? What shares should he sell? Whom should he marry? Searching for light. Desperate to know what the future held for him.

Modern, sophisticated Japan. In the forefront of the latest technology yet its people desperately empty and looking for guidance and answers from ways as ancient as time itself. From what we could see that day, Hosea had summed it up perfectly when he said: 'they consult a wooden idol and are answered by a stick of wood' (Hos. 4:12).

The desire for a crystal ball is not confined to Asia. How many in the West believe that the position of the sun, moon, and planets set against the backdrop of stars at the moment they were born, somehow affect personality, career, love-life and future? How many turn to astrology for light on life's major decisions? Newspapers carry columns simply because astrology sells newspapers. To say that it works is only to say that there are a lot of credulous yet satisfied customers. It is both deceptive and even sinister.

There is no such thing as a crystal ball. God has given us His Word. In that Word we will find light for our path. But that in no way means we should abuse Scripture and treat it as if it were some kind of almanac on which to construct projections for our future. To trust to chance to find an isolated verse of Scripture for guidance is hardly different in principle from the businessman of Akabusa consulting his sticks.

God's Word is to be understood God's way. Play the devil's game of Russian roulette with Scripture and you could be in for a shock. Isolate a text from its context and it becomes a pretext. It is as I seek to understand the whole counsel of God and behave 'as a workman who does not need to be ashamed and who correctly handles the word of truth' (2 Tim. 2:15) that I discover His Word to be 'a lamp to my feet and a light for my path' (Ps. 119:105).

But has God not given us any intimation by which we can predict the future? Of course He has. We know that ultimately every knee will bow to Him as Lord. We know that Jesus is Lord of the earth. We know He is coming back again. And while He did not spell out exactly what would occur in the final countdown, there is a sense in which He did tell us when that would be.

During the last few years of our ministry in Java we lived in Jakarta. Security was an issue. So, when we went on holiday, we had to leave someone to look after our house. As Wagiono waved us off, he vowed solemnly that he would guard the property and we need have no worries.

Our destination was a small wooden house high in the mountains above the tea estates of West Java. However, the rains meant that the wooded hills were shrouded in a permanent mist, and although we were in the tropics, it felt cold. We were housebound. With nothing more than a few indoor games and books, our four energetic boys showed distinct signs of holiday fatigue. So, we made the decision to cut our losses and go off to one of the beaches on the south coast where it would be warm and dry

That involved heading back first to our home in Jakarta. As we drew up to the house, there were signs of mad activity. Wagiono rushed out nervously. Our sudden arrival had not been factored into his plans. The house was a scene of chaos.

Thinking he had another ten days, Wagiono had invited his family and friends from the village to spend a few days with him sampling the delights of the city. Beds were unmade. Extra beds were laid out on the stone floor. There were people in every room. We could hardly believe it. They had gone through all our cupboards and drawers and, as we were to discover later, had been quite generous in helping themselves to what they decided we no longer needed. The look on Wagiono's face had to be seen to be believed. His jaw dropped, and in that moment of truth he simply said: 'We didn't expect you.'

A modern enactment of Jesus' parable – and with it the warning 'so you also must be ready, because the Son of Man will come at an hour when you do not expect him' (Matt. 24:44).

Jesus did, then, say when He was coming back. It will be when we don't expect Him! That should be warning enough. And there is one further warning – we are not to speculate any further than that. 'No one knows about that day or hour, not even the angels in heaven, nor the Son, but only the Father' (Mark 13:32). We are to live and behave as those who expect Him to come at any minute. And as we look at current events in the world around us, we should be in a state of high alert.

Meanwhile, we are entrusted with the stewardship of the gospel. Jesus did not promise that things would get easier. Many false teachers promise prosperity and affluence for all those who follow Jesus. Jesus, however, painted a very different picture of what we might expect after His ascension. Life would become more difficult as His coming again drew nearer. He warned of false 'messiahs.' He warned of those who would deceive. He warned of civil and military unrest. He warned that: 'Nation will rise against nation and kingdom against kingdom.' He told us that we would be persecuted or even killed as His followers and that many would turn away from the faith and be deceived. 'Because of the increase of wickedness,' He said, 'the love of most will grow cold, but he who stands firm to the end will be saved'

(Matt. 24:4-14). Not exactly an endorsement for those who would proclaim a 'Prosperity Gospel'!

As to the future, God is not in the business of satisfying our curiosity. He wants our trust and obedience. The only way to treat Scripture if we want to find light for our path is to do what it says. If we get that right, we can trust Him to lead us to the place where He wants us to be. That is what it means to make Him our refuge.

'Blessed are all who take refuge in him' (Ps. 2:12). While judgment waits for those who continue in rebellion, happiness and joy are for those who 'kiss the son' and make Him their refuge. That is the positive word we are to take to the nations – the news of salvation and the news that true happiness and security are to be found in Jesus alone. To that end He has commissioned us to call all people everywhere to the 'obedience that comes from faith' (Rom. 1:5).

The Psalmist asked: 'When the foundations are being destroyed, what can the righteous do?' (Ps. 11:3). That was the question in Habakkuk's mind, as his world seemed to be collapsing all around him. He faced the threat of war and longed to know what would happen next. God did not tell him. But as he faced each tomorrow, he did so with a new conviction: 'the righteous will live by his faith.' (Hab. 2:4). Or, taking the reading in the NIV margin, 'the righteous will live by his faithfulness.'

'Faith', 'faithfulness', which? Both are correct. The word means both. As Today's English Version translates it: 'Those who are evil will not survive, but those who are righteous will live because they are faithful to God' (Hab. 2:4 GNT) Generally the word is translated as 'faithfulness' in the Old Testament. The twin aspects of trust and obedience always go together in Scripture.

'When the foundations are being destroyed, what can the righteous do?' (Ps. 11:3). Answer: they can go on going on in faithful obedience, being obedient and holding to the faithfulness of God. That is what it means to take refuge in God. That is what it means to fear God. That is the antidote to anxious fear we learn from the second Psalm: 'Blessed are all who take refuge in him' (Ps. 2:12).

What does the future hold? As a young missionary in my twenties, a verse from what has been called 'a Psalm for old age' gave me great assurance: 'In you, O LORD, I have taken refuge; let me never be put to shame' (Ps. 71:1). If He is truly my refuge, I will never be put to shame. That is the promise. As Matthew Henry comments on that verse 'God will never disappoint the hope that is of his own raising.' But that is not to say He always lets us know what we may have to face on the journey.

As pilgrims heading towards Jerusalem for the annual festival, the place where God had chosen to reveal Himself and meet with His people, it was not all plain sailing. Looking at the road ahead they were to discover that there were hills to climb and valleys to pass through. In one of the Psalms of ascent, Psalm 121, the pilgrim sounds a note of concern: 'I lift up my eyes to the hills, where does my help come from?' (Ps. 121:1).

There was good reason for his realism. Jerusalem itself, where he was headed to meet with God, was itself set on a hill. He was obviously thinking of that. But at the same time the hills that surrounded Jerusalem had a reputation. The robbers Jesus spoke of in His parable of the Good Samaritan were notorious. The streams and ravines, slippery. The jagged rocks, hard to walk over. Particularly difficult for the elderly. Not the kind of place to spend the night, alone. Daunting. Small wonder he asks, 'where does my help come from?'

It is then the confidence of his faith answers his fear:

My help comes from the Lord, the Maker of heaven and earth. He will not let your foot slip—he who watches over you will not slumber; indeed, he who watches over Israel will neither slumber nor sleep. The Lord watches over you—the Lord is your shade at your right hand; the sun will not harm you by day, nor the moon by night. The Lord will keep you from all harm—he will watch over your life; the Lord will watch over your coming and going both now and forevermore. (Ps. 121:2-8)

Like the Psalmist, as pilgrims, we too are marching to Zion – not to any physical temple, but 'looking unto Jesus, the author and finisher of our faith' (Heb. 12:2 KJV). For Jesus is God's temple where He meets and reveals Himself to us, 'for God was pleased to have all his fullness dwell in him … for in Christ all the fullness of the Deity lives in bodily form' (Col. 1:19; 2:9).

Living in Scotland we are familiar with mountains. Familiar too with the fact that it all depends where you are along the road as to how high they appear to be. Travelling north on the M9 motorway, there is a short stretch near Bannockburn where over the horizon in the middle of the road, it looks as if there could be Alpine peaks away in the far distance. But then as you drive a little farther along, the road sweeps down into the broad, flat valley plain with Stirling Castle rising up on a great rock to your right and the 'peaks' you thought you saw have levelled out into fairly innocuous hills. Of course, living in Scotland, you also know there are days when the mists make it well-nigh impossible to even see any mountains at all!

In our pilgrimage to the heavenly Jerusalem, there will always be hills to climb and valleys to walk through. But as to just how high and threatening they appear or pop out of the mists not only depends on not only where along the road we find ourselves but how well we have come to know and trust the one who 'watches over you.'

In our younger days we face the hills of what we are to study, how to pass our exams, what career to pursue, whom to marry. Then as the road winds on up through middle years the hills become matters of earning our livelihood, our career path, our marriage, our children's education, our finances, where to live, the mortgage, what friends to make, what hobbies to follow, what church to join, what commitments to undertake, the horizon gets crowded—stressful—threatening even. Then as the horizon draws nearer and 'when the keepers of the house tremble, and the strong men stoop, when the grinders cease because they are few, and those looking through the windows grow dim; …' (Eccles. 12:3) to use the picturesque language of Ecclesiastes, the hills begin to seem insurmountable – loss of mental agility, loss of friends, loss of hearing, loss of physical strength, failing ability, each day a day's march nearer home.

But Psalm 84 says:

> Blessed are those whose strength is in you, whose hearts are set on pilgrimage. As they pass through the Valley of Baka, they make it a place of springs; the autumn rains also cover it with pools. They go from strength to strength, till each appears before God in Zion. (Ps. 84:5-7)

The hills have become valleys in the poetry of the Psalms. The underlying confidence of faith and trust in the one who watches over them is the same. Some had to pass through the deserted valley of Baka to get to Jerusalem – a dry, arid region, a weary, 'weeping' place, but looking back over their journey they found that it was worth it in the end.

What joy for those whose strength comes from the LORD, who have set their minds on a pilgrimage to Jerusalem. When they walk through the Valley of Weeping, it will become a place of refreshing springs. The autumn rains will clothe it with blessings. (Ps. 84:5-6, NLT)

The journey of the pilgrim, even when it had to be through times of weeping, found the enabling grace of God to take one step at a time and discover themselves going 'from strength to strength.'

In Psalm 124 the pilgrims have finally reached Zion. They look back at all the hills and valleys of their pilgrimage and say: 'If the Lord had not been on our side … the flood would have engulfed us, the torrent would have swept over us, the raging waters would have swept us away … Our help is in the name of the Lord, the Maker of heaven and earth.'

When the Psalmist in Psalm 125 looks back at the path he has chosen the significance of those very mountains has taken on a whole new perspective. He says:

Those who trust in the Lord are like Mount Zion, which cannot be shaken but endures forever. As the mountains surround Jerusalem, so the Lord surrounds his people both now and forevermore. (Ps. 125:1, 2)

The mountains were all part of enabling the Lord to work His purpose for our pilgrimage. Even when we didn't understand why we had to climb them.

The point is we are not left alone to climb the hills or walk through the valleys. A day will come, if not here on earth, then when we see our Lord face to face, when looking back we will see the hills we had to climb and valleys we had to walk through are reminders of His faithfulness, protection and the experience of 'his own dear presence to cheer and to guide.'

In John Newton's words, written just four years before his death:[2]

> His love in time past
> Forbids me to think
> He'll leave me at last
> In trouble to sink:
> Each sweet Ebenezer
> I have in review
> Confirms his good pleasure
> To help me quite through.
>
> Since all that I meet
> Shall work for my good,
> The bitter is sweet,
> The medicine is food;
> Though painful at present,
> 'Twill cease before long,
> And then, oh how pleasant,
> The conqueror's song!

---

2. Newton, John, 'Begone, unbelief' (1803).

CHAPTER 15

Walking with a Limp

He gives strength to the weary and increases the power of the weak. – Isaiah 40:29

A heart attack?

Three o'clock in the morning. Chest thumping. Body tense. Bolt upright in bed. Shivering, despite the tropical heat. Panic. I felt I was dying.

Adèle woke up.

'Whatever's wrong?'

'Hold me … tight!'

And that's exactly what she did. And I didn't die – just in case you wondered. But it certainly wasn't a case of 'man flu'.

Some eighteen months before, we had been asked to leave Jakarta to join the staff at OMF's International Headquarters in Singapore. It was the third time they had asked me, and after much struggling and praying, we sensed that if we were to move on in our pilgrimage we should accept. So, we left Indonesia, albeit with heavy feet. As far as we were able to discern it was another matter of obedience and a step of faith.

Aspects of the new ministry were thrilling and fulfilling: field trips to destinations around Asia; opportunities to give Bible Readings at Field conferences; getting to visit and know many of our colleagues in other parts of Asia; that was all joy. Handling paperwork and living with others in the 'goldfish bowl' of the Mission Compound was not! Increasingly I was not so much living in the goldfish bowl as struggling to keep my head above its water. For several weeks, starting before any of my colleagues were around, I would rise to that dark, early cool of the tropical morning, fire up the coffee machine in the office and start work. But still the paperwork crumpled my mind. I was beginning to feel I was out of my depth. I was struggling. Was I the only one or were others on the team having the same problem? The stresses of living in the community and over the office were oppressive. Had I accepted to do 'a job too far?'

It was then that a letter from the UK suggested all was not entirely well with the schooling arrangements we had made back in the UK. The emotional pressure from that hit both of us below the belt. Was it another mistake to decide on setting the course of secondary schooling for our four boys at a boarding school back in the UK? It had been one of the hardest decisions we had ever had to make together. Had we got that wrong as well?

Medical tests proved I was not having a heart attack. It was a classic panic attack associated with overwork and burnout. I needed a break. Mercifully, we were to get that break. It was made possible for the whole family to have Christmas together in Singapore and, in discussion, the decision was taken for us to have a period of home leave before resuming duties.

As to when we might go back as an IHQ director was left open. The time at home gave us a special time together to take stock as a family. But always, in the back of our minds, was the question of the when and the what next as to the Lord's direction for us as a family.

We needed advice. And God used special friends to help us. The first was the man who had been the Overseas Director when Adèle and I came out to Singapore as new workers, more than twenty years earlier – Arnold Lea – a godly man who combined wisdom with sanctified common sense. Now retired, Parkinson's had slowed him down physically, but his mind was as sharp as ever. He listened carefully as we laid out all the circumstances we were facing at home and told of the stresses we had found trying to cope with the dynamics of trying to live and work on the Mission's compound. Something he understood only too well from firsthand experience.

'I think we would need supernatural guidance *not to return* to Singapore,' I ventured.

Thoughtfully he stayed very quiet for quite some time. His response, when it came after serious evaluation was in a brief but measured statement.

'I think it needs to be the other way around. With the natural guidance you have before you, you would need supernatural guidance *to return* to Singapore!'

Both of us sensed he was right. But the thought of *not* going back was uncomfortable for me. It seemed like an admission we had made a mistake to accept the appointment in the first place.

Deep down, both of us knew that he was seeing clearly what was staring us in the face but were reluctant to accept. So, we notified the Mission we would not be coming back. And with that, we stepped out of more than twenty-two years of security in the OMF family we so loved. Now we faced the uncertainty of not knowing what the next step might be. But God knew and in His providential care He knew precisely who He would bring across our path.

Years before I was a committed Christian, while still an engineering student with Ford Motor Company, part of its training for possible management and leadership, I was to be sent to the Outward-Bound School in Eskdale for character assessment and development.

The Outward-Bound school, at that time, was under the leadership of Eric Shipton, a famous mountaineer. Roy Greenwood was appointed to be my supervisor. Roy was a well-known name in the Himalaya community. He had won his spurs back in the 1950's, climbing some of the notorious peaks well over 23,000 feet – achieved climbing without oxygen! Small in stature but all muscle! He redefined the word 'tough.' Walking the fells with him was an inspiration but rope work and the serious business of rock climbing filled me with terror. Roy would take the lead up a rock face and then have to help me over my fears to follow. Even knowing he was belayed safely above didn't ease my fear and I lack both the build and the agility to shin up ropes. 'You *can* do it,' he would call down. 'There's nothing you *can't* do if you try!' And, finally, success. I made it to the top. He had me convinced and it had worked. While I never did get to enjoy rock climbing, I achieved a small measure of success. His 'can do' attitude rubbed off. His objective to install a degree of self-reliance and confidence had worked.

Fast forward twenty-five years or so. Eskdale was a distant memory. The decision not to return to Singapore had been made. We were on our first holiday, all together at last as a family in the Lake District. We introduced the boys to the joys of walking the fells around Lake Coniston. Then, on Sunday, we went to the local church. As the minister came out of the vestry to lead the worship I couldn't believe what I saw: it was Roy – or to give him his title, the Reverend Roy Greenwood – looking just as he had more than twenty-five years ago, apart from his white surplice.

The bond was immediate. Knowing the fells like the back of his hand he took time out with all of us for walks over the Old Man of Coniston and Weatherlam. Much to our delight he took us to explore some of the spooky old caves and mining tunnels – places generally off-limits to tourists. As we walked, he told me how he had come to Christ, studied theology and then been ordained to become an Anglican Vicar. His first parish was in one of his beloved Lakeland valleys – 'A parish with more sheep than parishioners,' as he described it. Then he told me of how, for nearly all of twenty years in that ministry, he had to battle with depression. A depression eventually diagnosed to be partly the result of damage to his system from the episodes of oxygen starvation he had suffered from his exploits in the Himalaya. The very thing that had earned him a name in the climbing fraternity had become his thorn in the flesh and brought him humbling and distress in his ministry.

As we walked and shared it was easy to tell him of my experience of burnout. I remember saying, not boastfully but trying to tell it as it had seemed to me, that up until that bad experience in Singapore, I didn't ever recall not being able to succeed at anything I put my mind to. I reminded him of the maxim he had given me at those times with him when I had wanted to chicken out. He looked me squarely in the face with his very penetrating eyes.

'David, I probably told you then that there isn't anything you can't do,' he said.

'What I ought to have said, and what I have had to learn the hard way in my ministry is that without Christ, I can't do anything!'

Roy confessed the experience of his first charge had made him feel a failure. But God had brought him through it to use his experience, humbling though it was, to bless others. I could identify. It reminded me of God's wrestling with Jacob.

Jacob must have been one hardy, muscular specimen. It is a matter of record that he was a strong man physically (Gen. 29:2, 10). His strong arms and powerful limbs were essential equipment to earn his living as he walked the rough hills, tending sheep. In his world physical strength was vital for success. And he was a success. But at the brook Jabbok God had to wrestle him to the ground before he could be the man God wanted him to be. Wounded and limping Jacob clung on to seek God's blessing; humbled to learn that it was not his strength God needed but his submission. Not his ability but his vulnerability.

God had touched him at the very point where he had been able to take it for granted that he was strong and agile. What had once enabled him to stride confidently over the rocks was now to be put out of joint. Touched by God, he could only walk with a limp. His self-confidence shaken. His weakness and crippling obvious to all who saw him. Made vulnerable for the rest of his life. The God who had promised to bless him, at one and the same time, had to disable him in order to enable him – the paradox of grace. From living by his wits, the strong, self-confident Jacob had to be made weak and walk with a limp. But the twisted twister, Jacob, clung on and by the paradox of the grace, was to become Israel – a prince with God (Gen. 32:22-32).

The paradox of grace – the brokenness by which we discover more of His fatherly love and sufficiency. Wesley speaks of it in the final verses of his hymn, 'Wrestling Jacob':

Come, O thou Traveller unknown,
whom still I hold, but cannot see . . .

Yield to me now, for I am weak,
but confident in self-despair;
speak to my heart, in blessings speak,
be conquered by my instant prayer.
Speak, or thou never hence shalt move,
and tell me if thy name is Love!

'tis Love! 'tis Love! Thou died'st for me!
I hear thy whisper in my heart!
The morning breaks, the shadows flee;
pure universal Love thou art:
to me, to all, thy mercies move;
thy nature and thy name is Love.[1]

Paul had to learn the lesson of that paradox through what he called, 'a thorn in my flesh':

> Therefore, in order to keep me from becoming conceited, I was given a thorn in my flesh, a messenger of Satan, to torment me. Three times I pleaded with the Lord to take it away from me. But he said to me, 'My grace is sufficient for you, for my power is made perfect in weakness.' Therefore, I will boast all the more gladly about my weaknesses, so that Christ's power may rest on me (2 Cor. 12:7-9).

It was the same paradox the exiles that returned from Babylon to rebuild the temple had to understand. They were going to have to do a great deal of backbreaking work on the masonry, but progress was not going to go ahead on the basis of their ability or strength: 'This is the word of the

---

1. Wesley, Charles, 'Come, O thou traveller unknown', 1742.

Lord to Zerubbabel: "Not by might nor by power, but by my Spirit," says the Lord Almighty' (Zech. 4:6).

With the natural unsanctified desire most of us have to be thought of as successful in our ministry, it is a hard lesson to take on board. Yet Jesus told us the secret and made it more than clear from the very start: 'No branch can bear fruit by itself; it must remain in the vine. Neither can you bear fruit unless you remain in me' (John 15:4).

Dependence in and on Him, not confidence in our abilities, must undergird the whole of our ministry, if we are to bear lasting fruit in His service. We were saved by grace, and it is only by grace that we are enabled to do 'the good works, which God prepared in advance for us to do' (Eph. 2:9-10). And no matter what titles we may be given, what positions we may hold, what frenetic activities we may fill our days with, nor how many accolades we may be given, we are to, ' ... build with care ... if anyone builds on this foundation using gold, silver, costly stones, wood, hay or straw, their work will be shown for what it is, because the Day will bring it to light. It will be revealed with fire, and the fire will test the quality of each person's work' (1 Cor. 3:10-15).

To build with care means we are to do God's work, God's way. And it is just as important that we learn to do God's work God's way, as it is that we ever seek to do it at all.

So, the saga moved on. It had been decided that we would stay home in the UK with our family. But what next? Where and what, not to mention, how?

Eric Alexander had long been a friend of ours since our days at the Glasgow Bible Training Institute. Some years earlier I had invited him out to do the Bible readings at our missionary field conference. Following on from that the pair of us had travelled through Java to hold seminars for Indonesian Pastors on expository preaching. Eric was the teacher. My job was to be his chauffeur, organise the conferences and act as his translator. Back in the UK, he was chairman of our OMF Scottish Council alongside being the minister of St Georges Tron, Glasgow. We chatted about possibilities for future ministry. Higher academic qualifications were now required for anyone wanting to qualify for a missionary visa in Asia. My professional engineering credentials were not worth much in the eyes of the Indonesian Government's Department of Religion! Not having any academic theological degree, I thought I should take the opportunity, being at home for a while, to study for one.

'Study? A great idea,' he said, 'and I tell you where you are going to do it. In my pulpit!'

I probably should have quoted the famous line from John McEnroe at Wimbledon from the previous year's court battles on the tennis court: 'You *cannot* be serious!' But he *was* and so I *did*.

Adèle and I loved living and raising our family in Indonesia. By the grace of God, we had come to be comfortable speaking Indonesian and for so many years all my experience as a Bible teacher and preacher was in that language. Indonesian congregations were generous and accepting and always ready to forgive this foreigner any quaint mistakes he might make. But preaching for the next five years in English in a large sophisticated city centre church in Glasgow was very different. Words and phrases refused to pour out easily in what ought to have been my mother tongue. I stumbled. My delivery was halting. I limped nervously up the pulpit stairs, totally unnerved by the sea of faces staring at me from the pews. It was humbling. This was my homeland and yet I was not in my comfort zone – I felt I was out of my depth.

Each time it was my turn to preach, the boys would see me off to the vestry door with a cheery, 'Good luck Dad!' (That always brought a smile. I knew what they meant. I thought maybe there was a smile on God's face, '… out of the mouths of babes …') The family was wonderfully supportive. But what my shaky legs told me was that without Him, anything I did would be totally worthless. Eric was a joy to work with. We shared a sense of humour. He was ever the great encourager. I'm sure he knew I was learning to walk with a limp though he never ever gave a hint if he did. It was of the Lord's gracious loving care to give all of us, as a family, that support through this stormy period of our pilgrimage.

One day I was sitting in a cafe in Edinburgh reading my Bible. I was about to face a grilling interview by a learned group of clerics, most of whom were just about to pick me over, peering like owls, over their half-moon spectacles to see if they would recommend my acceptance to the General Assembly of the Church of Scotland. I was reading Psalm 77. 'Your path led through the sea, your way through the mighty waters, though your footprints were not seen … ' (Ps. 77:19).

The words brought peace. As if pieces were beginning to fit into the jigsaw. No matter how lonely, difficult and painful the path, nor how daunting the prospect of the interview ahead, God had walked with us, every step of the way and it was surely inconceivable that He would leave us now. He had to teach me things not found in any curriculum. It was all part of the training. Reader, they accepted me!

We had taken a step in faith. We sensed that was what God asked us to do. If he had told me then that it would involve a wrestling match to put my 'hip' out of joint, I doubt I would have agreed. But he knew the danger of walking with a mistaken idea of who I thought I was. He knew I needed to learn to walk with a limp, face the sunrise one day at a time and find that His staff is there to lean on.

Even though I walk through the darkest valley,
I will fear no evil,
for you are with me;
your rod and your staff,
they comfort me. (Ps. 23:4)

Of His deliverance I will boast, till all that are distressed
From my example courage take and soothe
their griefs to rest.[2]

2. Psalm 34 – Tate and Brady: Paraphrase

CHAPTER 16

The God of Covenant Love

*Even when I am old and grey, do not forsake me, my God, till
I declare your power to the next generation, your mighty acts
to all who are to come.* – Psalm 71:18

One of the most unforgettable messages I have ever experienced came from the lips of a dying man. In his day the
godly Dr. Johnstone Jeffrey had been a Moderator of the
Church of Scotland. He had been invited to the lectern at
the front of the lecture hall in the old Glasgow Bible Training
Institute to give a word to the students.

As he stood in front of us, he looked elderly and was
clearly very frail. He opened his Bible and simply said that
he wanted to read his favourite Psalm to us, Psalm 139.
As he read, the sense of God's presence in the room was
palpable.

> O Lord, you have searched me
> and you know me.
> You know when I sit and when I rise;
> you perceive my thoughts from afar.
> You discern my going out and my lying down;
> You are familiar with all my ways. (Ps. 139:1, 2)

We were conscious of hearing that other still small voice. He finished and looked exhausted. He had our sympathy. We waited for his message. We wondered if he was strong enough. His message, when it came, consisted of three halting sentences, nothing more.

'Young people often have problems with guidance for the future.'

There followed a very long pause.

'God will always give you enough light to take one more step.'

Another long pause.

'Take that step!'

And with that, he sat down.

The silence was eloquent. We searched our hearts; we felt we were being searched; there we found unfinished business: weaknesses in our prayer life, disobedience, areas where we knew God wanted us to 'take that step.'

A week or so later Johnstone Jeffrey died. The message that came through his reading of that Psalm and those three sentences have lived on with me to this day.

All of that was more than fifty-eight years ago and it was what came to mind forcibly as we found ourselves facing retirement, wondering just what the next step for our ministry might be.

Retirement. Something the media likes to portray as the warm afterglow on the sunny uplands of life. An attractive dream? The end of the rainbow?

Not without some truth – but not the whole truth. The halting questions and the answering affirmations in Christina Rossetti's beautiful poetic metaphor of life as the struggle of a journey 'up-hill ... the whole long day,' echo with those who would seek to live the life of faith.

Does the road wind up-hill all the way?
Yes, to the very end.
Will the day's journey take the whole long day?
From morn to night, my friend.

But is there for the night a resting-place?
A roof for when the slow dark hours begin.
May not the darkness hide it from my face?
You cannot miss that inn.

Shall I meet other wayfarers at night?
Those who have gone before.
Then must I knock, or call when just in sight?
They will not keep you standing at that door.

Shall I find comfort, travel-sore and weak?
Of labour you shall find the sum.
Will there be beds for me and all who seek?
Yea, beds for all who come.[1]

It would be comfortable to think that as the pilgrim life progresses the incline might ease off some before we reach the 'resting place.' The language is deceptively simple yet captures the life experience of many godly men and women through the ages. It was the converted slave trader, John Newton, who wrote poignantly about his own uphill journey:

I asked the Lord that I might grow
In faith and love and every grace,
Might more of His salvation know,
And seek more earnestly His face.
'twas He who taught me thus to pray,
And He, I trust, has answered prayer,

---

1. Rossetti, Christina, (1830-1894), 'Up-Hill'.

But it has been in such a way
As almost drove me to despair.

I hoped that in some favoured hour
At once He'd answer my request
And, by His love's constraining power,
Subdue my sins and give me rest.

Instead of this, He made me feel
The hidden evils of my heart
And let the angry powers of hell
Assault my soul in every part.

Yea, more with His own hand He seemed
Intent to aggravate my woe,
Crossed all the fair designs I schemed,
Humbled my heart and laid me low.

'Lord, why is this,' I trembling cried;
'Wilt Thou pursue Thy worm to death?'
"tis in this way,' the Lord replied,
'I answer prayer for grace and faith.'

'These inward trials I employ
From self and pride to set thee free
And break thy schemes of earthly joy
That thou may'st find thy all in Me.[2]

There was a time in the life of John Henry Newman when sailing home from Italy he became very unwell. Becalmed somewhere between Palermo and Marseilles he was overwhelmed by illness and doubt. Homesick and with his mind in turmoil he penned a poem which in later days was to be made into a hymn:

---

2. Newton, John, 'Olney Hymns', 1779.

Lead, kindly Light, amid the encircling gloom
Lead thou me on;
The night is dark, and I am far from home,
Lead thou me on.
Keep thou my feet; I do not ask to see
The distant scene; one step enough for me.[3]

'One step enough for me?'

Enough! Really? Facing retirement, we wondered just what that step might be for us. We had often quoted those words from Rene Padilla's experience, 'God will not give you a map, but He will give you His hand,' when counselling missionary candidates stepping out in faith for service in Asia. Now we were about to face a time when we were going to need to know, more than ever, just how to grasp and be grasped by that hand and walk on uphill, one step at a time!

Of course, there are times when we can, and indeed we should, do as much as we can to look to the future and plan ahead, sensibly. But then there are other times when the way ahead is not that clear and we just don't know where another step along the road will lead. Just as when climbing the Scottish mountains in a mist, you don't know what's beyond the next cairn because you just can't see through the mist. And, of course, you won't ever get to know until you reach the next cairn. But if God has given enough light for the next step, then, in faith, the challenge is to have the courage to trust Him and take it!

We had retired to a beautiful home in Perth. There was a preaching ministry round several churches in Perthshire, walking holidays in the Lake District, and wonderful trips to Switzerland with our caravan to meet up with some of Adèle's Swiss relatives along with former OMF Colleagues. There were happy times with our children and grandchildren

---

3. Newman, John Henry, (1801-1890) 'The Pillar of the Cloud', 1883.

in Dundee and Glasgow. However, after a few years it was becoming more and more obvious that Adèle was having difficulties. Cooking became complicated. Writing letters, confusing. Knowing how to answer people's questions at Church, intimidating. Offering hospitality and accepting invitations out from friends, daunting. Deciding what to wear, a mammoth exercise fraught with repeated attempts to get it just right. And trying to remember names and faces or just even to find words, stressful and, at times, impossible.

As for most older people, past their three score years and ten, memory problems are nothing out of the ordinary. Yet somehow Adèle's memory problems were not at all ordinary. What was the next step going to be?

Probably none of us go through life without fears of one form or another. For Adèle it was fear of the slow cruel disease she had seen stealing away the life of her mother. She was becoming more and more afraid of suffering from the very thing she had feared the most, ever since we first met at college some fifty-seven years ago. Alzheimer's.

As retirement progressed, she became more and more dependent. It became increasingly obvious that when I was not around, she would become disorientated, anxious and distressed. So, the next step was to move to a new house – hopefully for one last time. We wanted to be nearer to our children. We left Perth for Dundee. That was the easy part. We were used to moving to a new house! What followed proved to be more delicate. When you suspect the very thing you fear the most, how can you find help to face it? And how, as one who is looking on, can you help the one you love to summon up the courage they need to face up to the very thing they fear without adding to their fears?

For some time, both of us tried to live as if nothing was out of the ordinary. But as time went on it became harder to ignore what was becoming obvious. Slowly Adèle herself became increasingly aware that things were not right. She was struggling. She wrestled, we both wrestled, and finally it was with real courage that she decided to share her fear with our doctor.

It is one thing to fear the beast, but another to be brave enough to be prepared both to name it and look it in the face. Yet, again, in the remarkable gentleness of our loving Shepherd, it seemed that once the psychologist and psychiatrist had confirmed a diagnosis of Alzheimer's, she was given an amazing sense of acceptance. Her condition was no longer the thing that could not be named – the elephant in the room. It had been named, and by the grace of God, the Great Physician gave her the strength to accept the very thing that had so long been the nightmare that haunted her. He tempered her fears with the balm of His peace. In a spirit of gentleness that was evident throughout her life she proved the truth that the Lord was with her. She had learned Paul's secret:

> Do not be anxious about anything, but in every situation, by prayer and petition, with thanksgiving, present your requests to God. And the peace of God, which transcends all understanding, will guard your hearts and your minds in Christ Jesus (Phil. 4:6-7).

From that day to the day the Lord finally took her to be with Him, more than six years later, the progression of the illness was slow but the outcome inevitable. Going out became more and more difficult. It was neither easy nor appropriate to go into explanations to folk outside the family circle. The loving support and understanding from within our family and closest friends were wonderful, but the reactions of some outside that circle to the very private and sensitive personal decisions we had to make was not so easy to handle. We had to learn to live with the fact that some clearly didn't, and probably wouldn't, ever be able to understand.

And it was inappropriate to go into lengthy explanations; a difficult time as our circle of life, and what we had imagined was going to be our ministry, narrowed.

But it was a time when we were having to learn that, facing the prospect of what lay ahead, no matter how frightening, our loving heavenly Father would somehow use it for our good – to make us more like Jesus (Rom. 8:28-29). The important thing was to allow Him to do that in us and for us and even to each other. We had to learn to handle any uncomfortable thoughts we might have about what others might be thinking about us!

Fathers often disappoint and fail in our fallen sinful world. When Jesus taught us when we pray to say; 'Our Father,' He wanted us to know what it means to be able to call God our father. Human fathers fall short of the ideal, but God is not like an imperfect human father. He is the perfect pattern of what a true father should be. As Paul says, all fatherhood on earth derives its pattern from Him.[4] It is not the other way around.

Walking the life of faith should teach us that as our loving father all His ways are love even when we don't understand. Throughout our life and ministry, we had many experiences of that. We knew that God is love and all that He does He does in His love. But that does not mean we are the ones to decide to define what His love should be or how we should experience it in our lives. To do that would be to make ourselves judge and jury.

God's assurance to the prophet Isaiah is a beautiful reminder of His fatherly love for us even to grey hairs and the possible experience of failing mental powers as we grow older:

---

4. Ephesians 3:14-15. For this reason I kneel before the Father [The Greek for family (*patria*) is derived from the Greek for father (*pater*)], from whom every family in heaven and on earth derives its name].

Can a woman forget her sucking child, that she should not have compassion on the son of her womb? Yea, they may forget, yet will I not forget thee. Behold, I have graven thee upon the palms of my hands; thy walls are continually before me (Isa. 49:15-16).

In the words of the hymn:

> A debtor to mercy alone,
> Of covenant mercy I sing ...
>
> The work which His goodness began,
> the arm of His strength will complete;
> His promise is Yea and Amen,
> and never was forfeited yet.
> Things future, nor things that are now,
> nor all things below or above,
> Can make Him His purpose forgo,
> or sever my soul from His love.
>
> My name from the palms of His hands
> eternity will not erase;
> Impressed on His heart it remains,
> in marks of indelible grace.
> Yes, I to the end shall endure,
> as sure as the earnest is given;
> More happy, but not more secure,
> the glorified spirits in Heaven.[5]

Questions? Of course, there were. Many! Yet all through those years came a deep conviction that the Lord knew what He could trust us with. One of the Puritan writers wrote that in the battle of life whatever arrow, from whatever source, by the time it has been allowed access to our lives, has become the Lord's will for us. We believed that to be true. 'In His will,

---

5. Augustus Montague Toplady (1740-1778), 'A debtor to mercy alone'.

is our peace,'[6] and therefore sickness or health, poverty or riches, the very things we promised to weather when we took our marriage vows, are not works of chance but all came to us from His fatherly hand. Truths so beautifully expressed in the Heidelberg Catechism.[7]

The Psalmist in his distress said: 'My soul refused to be comforted' – but then he gets a new perspective on his problems when he says, 'then I thought, "to this I will appeal: the years of the right hand of the most high. I will remember the deeds of the Lord ... "' (Ps. 77:1,2; 10-12). He looks back to God's saving acts and His faithfulness and finds comfort. He remembers God's covenant with His people; He saves; He delivers; He is faithful to His promises; He does not change when our circumstances and experiences of life change! There lies our confidence that His love will not fail us in the time of stress. His Covenant Love never changes. It does not 'alter when it alteration finds.'[8] So we can move forward in confidence as Newton put it:

> His love in time past forbids me to think
> He'll leave me at last in trouble to sink;

---

6. Dante, *The Divine Comedy*.

7. Williamson, G. I., *The Heidelberg Catechism* (Phillipsburg, NJ: P&R Publishing, 1993), p. 48.

Q 27 What do you mean by the providence of God?

A: The almighty and everywhere present power of God; whereby, ... food and drink, health and sickness, riches and poverty, yea, all things come, not by chance, but by his fatherly hand.'

Q 28 What does it profit us to know that God has created, and by his providence still upholds all things?

A: That we may be patient in adversity; thankful in prosperity, and with a view to the future may have good confidence in our faithful God and Father that no creature shall separate us from his love, since all creatures are so in His hand, that without His will they cannot so much as move.'

8. Shakespeare – Sonnet 116: 'Let me not to the marriage of true minds ...'

> Each sweet Ebenezer I have in review,
> Confirms His good pleasure to help me quite through.[9]

Alzheimer's has famously been called 'the long goodbye.' Watching as slowly your life partner recedes from being the person you once knew to be your dearest friend, mother of your children and life companion, is a grief I find utterly beyond the capacity of words to describe. It is a heart-rending unresolved grief. As a psychiatrist friend, who had cared for her husband for many years in his dementia, put it: 'You spoke in your letter of grieving as if bereaved and I can so understand that. In my worst moments I felt neither a wife nor a widow ... ' But God is close to us,[10] even in the loneliness and pain of bereavement.

I was asked at that time as to how I felt. I only share what I wrote then if perhaps it might help anyone reading this who is facing a similar experience with his or her loved one. I wrote:

> It is not easy to explain and folks looking on from the outside just would not be able to understand what it means to be living with someone who is, at this stage, defined clinically as being at the 'moderate stage' of the illness. The hardest thing of all is at the deepest of levels – our relationship as man and wife and the mutual comfort of meaningful discussion and dialogue of companionship – the fundamental of any marriage.
>
> Some illnesses, like cancer, we would all dread but even that would be something we could face together as a couple. We could talk about ways to try to fight it and still know the meaningful intimacy of debate,

---

9. Newton, John, 'Begone unbelief', 1779.

10. Acts 17:27-28 ... he is not far from any one of us. 'For in him we live and move and have our being.'

discussion and relationship. We could talk about it and share our fears but the progress of Adèle's Alzheimer's no longer allows for that. There is no way I can talk to her about problems – she will only register distress and fail to understand really what I am saying or get distressed. There is now no way to discuss what we can do for the best. No way to discuss what course of action we should take or what decisions we should make. That, I find, is one of the hardest things to live with. And it means, in some way I have to try and sense what is in Adèle's best interests even when I cannot hope for a rational answer from her.

The problem is that whatever our public face may seem to be – and Adèle can almost seem normal when people greet her socially – it is just not really possible to explain the mental and emotional strain of living with what in some ways feels like a living bereavement – and even just expressing that doesn't begin to tell the half of the story.

Someone said I have to learn to manage a 'balancing act' between my needs and Adèle's, but it is not a 'balancing act' as such but rather a situation where the 'one flesh' finds itself being irreversibly and painfully torn apart in slow motion – not something anyone who hasn't passed this way can be expected to understand. Someone, trying to be nice, said; 'Oh yes, I understand, I had a relative who has Alzheimer's' – they meant well, but their experience and ours could not be more radically different. When it is your life's love and companion (your other half – your better half) who is fading away – dying by instalments – that is not the same thing as dealing with a 'relative' in the family.

There are times when Adèle is not clear as to who I am – a good loveable (I trust) friend and carer for sure – and I am grateful for that. More often than not she seems to confuse me with her brother Len. That makes the experience of the illness within a marriage relationship to be of an entirely different order. The experience and my emotional reactions to it are not something I can verbalise. And how Adèle for her part feels about where she is at in terms of her own inner consciousness is not something I can know because she cannot tell me. And yet I have to try and sense where she is at. I have to monitor her emotional reactions. Her perception of reality.

And speaking of that perception of reality, there was a time when we might watch the news, a DVD, or some other programme on TV but now I realise that when the TV is on she confuses what she sees with the realities of where she is. That narrows down what it is 'safe' for her or for us to watch together. The News broadcasts which portray tense situations have her very agitated and distressed …

It was around the time that I wrote those words, that a friend of ours in North America sent us a small book by Robertson McQuilkin, who for twenty-two years had been the president at Columbia International University. His wife had the same form of dementia as Adèle and in the book he described the moment he made the decision to resign his position as President to care for her.

Some questioned the wisdom and appropriateness of resigning his position for her. Was he not leaving a strategic and important work and losing wider influence he could have had for the kingdom?

He wrote one of the most winsome and Christlike explanations of his reasoning, and most importantly of the privilege of his first and last covenant calling to his wife. It was both a comfort and a challenge to me and I realised God was giving me enough light to take the next step – Adèle's full time care. He said:

The decision to come to Columbia was the most difficult I had to make. The decision to leave, though painful, was one of the easiest … Let me explain.

My dear wife, Muriel, has been in failing mental health for about twelve years. So far, I have been able to carry both her ever growing needs and my leadership responsibility at Columbia. But recently it has become apparent that Muriel is contented most of the time when she is with me, and almost none of the time when I am away from her. It is not just 'discontent.' She is filled with fear – even terror – that she has lost me, and always goes in search of me when I leave home. So, it is clear to me that she needs me now, full-time.

Perhaps it will help you understand if I share with you what I shared in Chapel at the time of the announcement of my resignation. The decision was made, in a way, forty-two years ago when I promised to care for Muriel 'in sickness and in health … till death us do part.' So, as I told the students and faculty, as a man of my word, integrity has something to do with it. But so does fairness. She has cared for me fully and sacrificially all these years. If I cared for her for the next forty years, I would not be out of her debt. Duty, however, can be grim and stoic. There is more: I love Muriel. She is a delight to me – her childlike dependence and confidence in me, her warm love, occasional flashes of wit I used to relish so, her happy spirit and tough resilience in the face of her continual distressing frustration. I don't have to care for her. I get to! It is a high honour to care for so wonderful a person.[11]

You have to wonder if Robert and Muriel, as they pledged and affirmed their love to each other in covenant before God and the congregation of His people, in the first flush

11. McQuilkin, Robertson, *A Promise Kept*, Tyndale House Publishers, 1998, p. 21-23.

of youth, full of joy, with health and strength and physical beauty, could ever have pictured having to face this moment in their lives? If they had, might they have retreated in fear from that picture of themselves in their latter days?

So, for us the 'the Next Step' was clear. For me it was: 'I love … Adèle … I don't have to care for her. I get to. It is a high honour to care for so wonderful a person.' For Adèle it had to be to accept the very thing she had so long feared and trust that I would continue to do my utmost, humanly speaking, to love and care for her, 'till death us do part.'

In our entire ministry together, she had always been my memory for faces and names! Now remembering names was quite beyond her. A glimpse of the face of a friend we may have met on our travels many years ago would come back to her mind suddenly, and she would think that they were somewhere in the house. The result of our nomadic life and an open home, meant that at such times she experienced the powerful sense, but ill-informed, that some form of hostess duty was expected of her and she would become quite ill at ease and perplexed, not knowing how to do what she thought she ought to be doing. Adèle loved exercising the gift of hospitality. Now she could no longer open the home; our world began to shrink.

Finally, one evening while watching the news, she asked me, 'Are you going to send me home?' Of course, my immediate answer was to reassure her and say, 'But this is home!' But although she smiled sweetly, my answer made no sense. Inexorably the illness progressed. She began to lose all concept of where home was. Gradually she even began to wonder who I was. At times she would look at me quizzically and ask, 'Do you know David Ellis?'

Early one morning the doorbell rang and our neighbour from across the road stood on the doorstep, having found Adèle shivering in her night clothes far down our street refusing to be led back to the house. With Adèle's brother and his wife from Canada staying overnight with us we had forgotten to lock the front door. Adèle, who would frequently get up in the night and walk about, had managed to get out of the house and wander down the road. I ran outside and down to the next bend in the road to find her holding hands with our neighbour's wife, then she came back home with me. This was not the first time this had happened.

I select these few vignettes from so many similar stories through the years, leaving out others which it would be too painful to relate; quoted, not because they were dramatic and exceptional but because they typified the routine of our lives through those days. Domestic scenes made poignant by their very ordinariness and our seeking to understand God's hand on both our lives. We knew Him to be the faithful and loving Lord who had delivered us from many of our fears in many strange and exceptional dangers. Somehow, we had to see that He was still with us in this, the mundane and wearying day-to-day experience He had permitted for our pilgrimage. He is the God of the big picture, raising up and bringing down nations and kingdoms, but now we had to discover that He is not silent or far away when we need Him more than ever. We were grappling with the intimate needs of our frail and failing bodies and minds, but He was true to His promise: 'I will never leave you or forsake you!' Or as the Classic Amplified Bible (AMPC) highlights the impact and emphasis of the text in the original:

> … for He [God] Himself has said, I will not in any way fail you nor give you up nor leave you without support. [I will] not, [I will] not, [I will] not in any degree leave you helpless nor forsake nor let [you] down (relax My hold on you)! [Assuredly not!][12]

---

12. Hebrews 13:5 – 'Amplified Bible Classic Edition' cf. Deuteronomy 31:6.

Did the Lord have to take us through this path in our marriage that we might come to understand, at a much deeper level, the nature and meaning of His Covenant Love for us? Christ, as our great bridegroom saw and knew from before the world was made, exactly what it was going to cost Him to establish that covenant relationship with us as His bride. It would cost Him His life. All that was something we thought we knew – but to what extent was it embedded in our hearts?

Towards the end, when her illness was getting to be more than we could handle as a family, we had to face up to the reality that she needed professional care. And so, with the advice and help of the family, and in the goodness of God we found a place nearby in the community. The staff there made it a loving home. Being the gentle, gracious and godly person she had always been, they did not find it hard to love her. I was able to visit her most days for the final two years of her life and whenever we would sit together on a sofa, read the scriptures and pray she was calm and at peace. Often, I suspect, she mightn't have been exactly sure as to who I was. But there were just one or two occasions when I would arrive and see her face light up with a beautiful smile of recognition. The sense of joy of being able to lock eyes with the dearest face in all the world on such days was an unforgettable experience. A memory that even now moistens my eyes.

But we must see through our tears and look into the face of Christ. And it is, as His face comes into focus, that we discover, in greater depth, the health-giving fear of the Lord. He is the bridegroom who has made, and will keep, His covenant promises to us as His bride no matter what changes in us. He doesn't love us because He saw us as warriors who would hold the course. He did not choose us because we might become characters you write legends about (Eph. 1:4). None of us dare claim to be heroes that merit His love. Our doubts and fears and failing powers may surprise us. They do not surprise Him or weaken one billionth part of a percent His willingness to love us to the end and help us along the road as it winds uphill 'the whole long day.' His covenant of love stands on an unshakeable foundation – He gave Himself for us. He loves us and redeemed us with His own life's blood.

Throughout Scripture God describes His relationship with His people in terms of a marriage relationship. Marriage is defined as being between a man and a woman; an analogy of the covenant relationship we have with our heavenly bridegroom, Christ. That is why it is so very special, a covenant promise establishing our identities within the relationship we have to one another as husband and wife, never to be entered into without serious commitment. Doubts, fears, frailty, illness, pain and weakness do not change that relationship. That is the crowning glory of marriage, as God designed it, that it survives and holds firm no matter what winds He may allow to blow upon it! God gave marriage to us to be a picture of His forever-husband love to us!

> Husbands love your wives, just as Christ loved the church and gave himself up for her … the two will become one flesh. This is a profound mystery – but I am talking about Christ and the church. (Eph. 5:25, 31-32)

Despite the adjustments we had to face in the last years of our marriage, one thing never changed – our relationship. Adèle was my wife; I was her husband! Before God, and before the law of the land, we had entered into the covenant of marriage and made our vows to one another. It was that mutual promise that underwrote the bond between us. Before God we were man and wife. One flesh. Our identities did not alter on account of her illness.

And, whether or not she was able to understand it, as her mind began to shut down, it was that covenant love into which we entered before God and our Indonesian brothers and sisters in the Javanese Church at Salatiga, more than fifty years ago, which was the assurance that I would always love, care and provide for her for as long as I was able to look after her.

As believers we are 'in Christ.' And Christ lives in us by His Spirit. It is through His indwelling presence we are empowered to live, for He 'is able to do immeasurably more than all we ask or imagine, according to his power that is at work within us' (Eph 3:20). No matter what we experience, how we feel or whatever happens to us in this world, that is what defines our relationship to God. Being 'in Christ' has become our identity.

Adèle committed herself to Christ in her teenage years. She had been born again and knew the truth that 'if anyone is in Christ, the new creation has come' (2 Cor. 5:17). She, by the grace of God, was a new creation living in a new relationship to God. The identity that defined her was that she was 'in Christ,' the identity that was described by the Apostle Paul when he said: 'I have been crucified with Christ and I no longer live, but Christ lives in me. The life I now live in the body, I live by faith in the Son of God, who loved me and gave Himself for me (Gal. 2:20).

She walked with God and knew the secret that so many of the Lord's people have discovered: 'the glorious riches of this mystery, which is Christ in you, the hope of glory' (Col. 1:27). People today have become obsessed with the question of identity and, of course, as you watch the sad progression of someone with Alzheimer's, the question of identity inevitably rises in your mind. But for Adèle we knew the wonderful truth that, being 'in Christ,' that identity of hers would never change.

That's who she was. That's who she still is. Despite her frailty, that identity was never lost – it remained unaffected by what she was able to feel or understand. Nothing could alter it. And it was with that very identity she was welcomed with open arms into the 'resting place.' Towards the end of her road, when all her human resources were depleted and her mind had all but closed down, what she could not now understand any more didn't matter. Her Lord's resources were more than enough for her. She was His.

Christ never promised immunity from suffering and times of anxiety. None of us go through life without fears, a fear that our faith might fail in the last years under severe testing, a fear of persecution, a fear of being challenged to deny our faith, a fear of suffering, a fear of ill health, a fear of pain, a fear of poverty, a fear of bereavement, a fear of loneliness – the list could go on and on and on. But if our trust is in Christ then, being 'in Christ,' we are secure in the promise of His unchanging Covenant Love. 'I will never leave you or forsake you!' The one, who sees us as His bride and reveals Himself to us as our husband, will never abandon us. Never – not ever!

It is three years ago since Adèle passed away. We were happily married for fifty-two years. For all of us life has its good days and bad days, its massive reversals, its domestic day-to-day traumas, and everything in between. But for believers none of that changes who we are in our relationship and identity as those who are 'in Christ.' It isn't dependent on how we feel nor is it destroyed by anything that life might throw at us. It is an identity and relationship based on His Covenant Love – His marriage commitment to us. And that is the guarantee we have, as followers of Christ, that He will keep us safe and secure as His own to the very end of the way.

Yes, I to the end shall endure,
As sure as the earnest is given;
More happy, but not more secure,
The glorified spirits in Heaven.[13]

As the Good Shepherd says of His lambs: 'I give them eternal life, and they shall never perish; no one will snatch them out of my hand' (John 10:28).

What an extraordinary gospel! Christ left heaven to make me His bride. Beautiful in His eyes! I am loved, not because of anything in me but because of the beauty of who He is – for God is love. If being 'in Christ' defines my identity, then nothing can make me unattractive in His eyes. Nothing can separate me from His love:

> If God is for us, who can be against us? He who did not spare his own Son, but gave him up for us all – how will he not also, along with him, graciously give us all things? Who will bring any charge against those whom God has chosen? … For I am convinced that neither death nor life, neither angels nor demons, neither the present nor the future, nor any powers, neither height nor depth, nor anything else in all creation, will be able to separate us from the love of God that is in Christ Jesus our Lord (Rom. 8:31-39).

Incredible? Yes! But glorious gospel truth!

And that is what it means to *fear* God. That is the fear that can drive out every other fear. And if that sounds a lot like *love* God, that's because in the end they come to the same thing.

Of that love Paul says: 'For now we see only a reflection as in a mirror; then we shall see face to face. Now I know in part; then I shall know fully, even as I am fully known'

---

13. Augustus Montague Toplady (1740-1778), 'A debtor to mercy alone'.

(1 Cor. 13:12). Throughout her life, Adèle knew that love 'in part.' Now she knows it fully, even as she is 'fully known'.

Let us bow before Him. May He, in His grace, help us come to know the wonder of His Covenant Love in greater depth so that the very peace of God, that passes understanding, might keep our hearts and minds in Christ Jesus (Phil. 4:6-7).

Through all the changing scenes of life,
In trouble and in joy,
The praises of my God shall still
My heart and tongue employ.
O make but trial of His love;
Experience will decide
How blest are they, and only they,
Who in His truth confide.

Fear Him, ye saints, and you will then
Have nothing else to fear;
Make you His service your delight.
Your wants shall be His care.[14]

God will always give you enough light to take one more step – take that step!

---

14. Brady, Nicholas (1659-1726), and Tate, Nahum (1652-1715), 'Through All the Changing Scenes of Life'.

CHAPTER 17

The Valley of the Shadow

Heaven was in her, before she was in heaven. – Sibbes

The book needs one final chapter to round out the story of those final years of Adèle's pilgrimage. At her thanksgiving service, David Robertson, our minister, along with our son John, were able to add richer colour to the story of Adèle's life and testimony than I could ever paint. David writes:[1]

Last week 200 people from many different parts of the land gathered in St Peters to celebrate the life of an extraordinary woman. I know that funerals are nowadays often styled as celebrations and the phrase can become somewhat clichéd. But this one was. And here is the interesting thing – it was not primarily a celebration of the life of Adèle Ann Ellis, but rather a celebration of the goodness and glory of God in her life. It was, for all who were there, an extraordinary occasion.

It is hard to describe what happened. We sang 'See, What a Morning,' 'There is a Hope that Burns Within my Heart,' 'In Christ Alone' and 'How Good is the God we Adore.' We prayed. We read the Scriptures. Her brother John MacBeath and her son John gave tributes. Sinclair Ferguson brought

---

1. Revd. David Robertson @ theweeflea.com.

the Word to us. We ate and drank together afterwards. But that is only a description of the outline.

Adele was born on the 27th of April 1936 and died on the 10th of November 2016. She was a mother of four boys (John, Graham, Mark and Paul), had a double first in languages, spoke Italian, French, Indonesian and was a woman of quite remarkable intelligence. Married to David, former Associate Minister of St George's Tron and OMF International leader, their life was one of struggle, joy, service and great support of one another. The bare facts of her life serve only to act as a container to describe the richness of it …

Adèle was described by Sinclair as 'the woman of the book.' Because she knew the author and loved Him. Psalm 23 seems an almost too obvious passage of Scripture to read at a funeral, but it was so incredibly applied. When she and David became members in St Peters, Adele was already in the advancing stages of severe dementia. Suddenly the words of the Psalm struck home in a new way, 'Yea, though I walk through the valley of the shadow of death, I will fear no evil.'

Dementia is most certainly the valley of the shadow… and yet even in that the Lord was with her. No – perhaps especially in that the Lord was with her. She may have forgotten many things, but He never forgot her.

But now she is out of the valley. She is on the ultimate mountaintop, at the ultimate feast. That is why we celebrated. As Christians there is a joy in death (as well as real sorrow) that the world just cannot grasp. You need to be in Christ, in order to understand even a little of the beauty of being with Christ.

My hope and prayer are that those of the 200 who were in St Peters last Thursday, who are not yet in Christ, will at least have had a taste of what that might mean.

'Heaven was in her, before she was in heaven' (Sibbes).

The following is the tribute that my good friend John paid to his mum. It is one of the most beautiful things I have ever heard:

Most of you will have known my mother, as Adèle. I have known her all my life – coming up for fifty years – and I have never once called her that. I am not alone. Four people here have only ever called her mum, four more have come to call her mother through marriage, and ten more have only ever called her granny. Some relationships are so profound we use the relational word over against any other and instead of the proper name, but this is familiar to the Christian. We read, 'Then Jesus answered, "when you pray say, 'our father which art in heaven …'"' As far as we know even angels can't say that.

Perhaps as the result of that life-defining relationship, no child can really conceive of their parents' existence before they were born. Even as I grew into adulthood, I heard stories like my Uncle John's of my mother's adventures before we came to be part of her story and I heard them with a degree of wonder, like news from another country and another time, news of a life lived large. She seems to me to have lived a nomadic and exotic life. Registering her death with the registrar in City Square last Friday, and looking at her birth certificate, I was struck by the thought that the town in which her birth was registered, Leopoldville, doesn't even exist anymore (that's modern-day Kinshasa). Even the Belgian Congo no longer exists.

Betty and I went with David and Shona, two of her grandchildren to Southeast Asia, to see one of the places where I had lived and not one building was left standing of all that I remembered. This is trivial in comparison: for my mother, the child of missionary parents with their hearts set on pilgrimage, she had no permanent home, and even her country of birth has been renamed.

I knew of her double first honours degree in languages. But her intelligence never found expression through one-upmanship or showy display, but in the flashes of wit and in the deep, deep love of literature and poetry, which she passed on to us. I don't know if it was a grief to her that we all seemed to follow our Father 'genetically' into technical and scientific subjects and left a love of literature to our private and personal lives.

Shona remembers at family gatherings in the house in Perth how she used to slip away from the grown-ups to the bookcase upstairs. She knew it wouldn't be long before granny noticed a child was missing from the gathering and would set out just as quietly, find Shona at the top of the stairs, and begin to read to her.

Above the head of her bed at Meigle Country House was a copy of 1 Corinthians 13, done in her own beautiful calligraphy. Paul says there that love does not draw attention to itself. For all her great learning and intelligence, Mum moved with an easy grace through the lives of those she loved and who loved her ... never drawing attention to that hinterland of learning and reading. In fact, though intelligent and quick of mind, she was generally awful at telling jokes, but laughed with genuine delight at everyone else's – happy that they, not she, was in the limelight when they delivered the punchline.

All her life she was surrounded by boys: first by three brothers, and no sisters, then a husband, then four boys. God perhaps preserved the gentleness of women, one of His tenderest gifts to her till her later life in the form of the nursing care she received at Meigle Country House in the last two years of her life. There, despite the cruelty of the Alzheimer's, she loved and was loved. When dad could no longer care for her as he wished, Rhona and Karen and their team – round-the-clock – exemplified to us the *imago dei* – the image of God.

There is a line in *Hamlet* I often think of when I think of my father's love for my mother. Hamlet, speaking of his dead father's love for his mother says of the murdered King: "so excellent a king … So loving to my mother that he might not beteem[2] the winds of heaven visit her face too roughly." When I think that the man – who loved his wife that well – could be confident to leave her in the care of the staff at Meigle, I know it says more than words ever could about how highly we all as a family esteemed the loving, caring, patient, homely, gentle ethos of that place.

Sitting in my father's dining room on the morning of the day she died, Mark, Graham and I all retrieved at the same time one common memory. We were on the beach on a family holiday in Java playing in the sand dunes when my mother quite unreasonably and with no warning whatsoever began to do cartwheels. Balance and poise and athleticism perfectly executed despite the fact, that unless she practiced them in secret, she must not have done a cartwheel for decades. All of us boys were so surprised we stopped doing what we were doing, abandoned our play and dropped our mouths wide open. Such was my surprise that I remember exactly what she was wearing at the time. Slightly flared white 70s trousers with an Indonesian Batik top. None of the brothers at the time mentioned this to each other.

In the days after mum died I received a lot of lovely, thoughtful texts, and one very dear friend said your mother is walking with her Lord in the cool of the evening of Eden … and I'm sure she is – sometimes – but I rather more pictured her doing cartwheels of utter, exploding, uncontainable, happiness in His presence!

Sharing just that one cameo leads me to ask; have you ever been to a funeral of someone you loved and thought

---

2. 'Beteem' – to allow, to permit, to suffer.

that the eulogy was adequate? I don't think so … in fact the more you loved them and the better you knew them, the more inadequate you probably thought the eulogy. Why? Because I think our expectations are understandable … but impossible. We want to see that person set free again in the eye of our imagination as they once were and, in a sense, we want, therefore, to see them again. And that isn't possible. It is beyond the craft of even the best wordsmith. We can't adequately describe another human being … Not really … not in that ultimate sense …

So I remember the family feasts and her amazing hospitality; and I remember FHB (Family Hold Back). I remember when she declared 'Manners Maketh Man Weak' when she grew frustrated in her entirely reasonable efforts to tame four feral children – disgusted by our table manners – she decided to feed us our meal off newspaper spread on the dining room table to illustrate the shoddy consequences of our actions – and who should turn up that mealtime but one of our uncles to introduce us to his new fiancée! He couldn't stop laughing and the grandeur of the lesson was entirely lost!

I remember 101 recipes for mince and the fact that mum earned so many 'frequent flyer miles' with the butcher that he gave her one free pound with every ten. I remember she then tried to vary our diet with liver and onions – which we hated … But I remember how we always ate together at table … I remember her terrible sense of direction and her faulty personal thermostat – wearing six, seven or more layers, even in the height of summer. And I remember all the amazing bread she made, daily, in a rusty old box oven – literally – lifted and placed on top of the stove in Jakarta, three legs supported by the dodgy gas ring and the fourth balanced on a cork.

I remember the letters. How many letters she wrote, often illustrating them with watercolours of life or Tintin or Narnian characters. Only one thing I don't remember: I cannot ever recall her complaining. Ever. About anything. She was godly, and gracious and generous and gentle … but I have always known, ever since the Alzheimer's disease began its long, slow theft, what memory would linger longest and be most defining of her. I remember that apart from I think one week; literally perhaps seven nights when I was ill and could not sleep, that every morning; any morning, whatever the day, whatever the time … when I came down to breakfast I found mum seated at the dining table reading her bible. There were no exceptions I can remember apart from two weeks on one holiday in the Lake District in a house with wooden window shutters when she wasn't woken by the light (she was a very light sleeper) and slept in, something I didn't know she could do … no exceptions. There she was reading her Bible.

When I was a teenager in the 80s, I sent off for a get rich quick book. It was rubbish and I threw it away. But – with some embarrassment – I do remember doing it, I thought nothing more of it until many, many years later I found that mum had kept an A5 trifold flyer from that mailing and used it as a bookmark in her bible. It had the firm's slogan on the front and read 'the secret of real wealth; how to quietly accumulate real wealth and retire rich.' Well – better than those yuppy salesmen realised, she did quietly accumulate real wealth and retired rich.

You will have recollections and profound memories I have omitted, and I would have included many domestic and mild memories you might have bettered – There are many more examples of her godliness and faith … But even if I shared a CV – a kind of catalogue of the years – that wouldn't do it. You will have heard the kind of thing that the average human spends twenty-five years sleeping and so on. Well, I have reflected that in our life together as a family, mum spent thirty-six months pregnant, twelve years dealing with toddlers under three and so on ... but there's one statistic in this slightly strange way of looking at things, that is sobering ...

She – that is, both my parents – lived through a total of thirty years of separation from their four children, between 1972 and 1984 (11, 8, 6, 5). Twice a year for all those years, with a tender mother's heart, she said goodbye to four children going away to boarding school, why? Because her Lord and Master asked it of her, and she knew Him well enough to know that He would take care of her children for her.

I remember the joy of returning home, as the taxiing aeroplane reached its hold on the Jakarta tarmac, we could always see her amongst the waving crowd with a large white square; a white terry nappy kept for the purpose. And we always came home to our favourite food which was always pumpkin pie ... And all holiday she dropped everything and, presumably every preference of her own and every wish for privacy, to create a secure world and family subculture that represented ultimate security and comfort.

My parents shared and passed onto us the love of C.S. Lewis' *Narnia* in the last chapter of the last book, *Farewell to Shadowlands* ... Part of which mum had written again in her beautiful calligraphy for my dad's 70th Birthday. Aslan speaks to the children;

'You do not yet look so happy as I mean you to be.'

Lucy said, 'We're so afraid of being sent away, Aslan.' ...

'Have you not guessed?' said Aslan ... Their hearts leaped, and a wild hope rose within them.

'There was a real railway accident,' said Aslan softly.

' ... all of you are – as you used to call it in the Shadow-lands – dead. The term is over: the holidays have begun. The dream is ended: this is the morning.'

Mum has reached the place where there is never any more separation. And, as she now knows all she needs to know about all God's providence in her life, she will be able to add the delight of praising Him that as Psalm 119 says, 'You are good and [everything you] do [is] good,' by sure and certain knowledge, not 'just' by faith, as we do. She will know why so many partings and separations were right and needed and the cascading good consequences that could be achieved no other way that came from them ...

But not because the 'joy of heaven' is an explanation. No: all that is needed is one glimpse of the Lamb on the throne, and all questions will vanish; just adoring Him she will know of course that 'He is good and all he does is good' ... Mum is experiencing that truth, and the truth, that Revelation 21:4 does not say He will send one of His angels with a Kleenex to mum, to wipe away every tear, but He Himself will do it.

Now I know that Mum is home, truly home, at the end of a life set on pilgrimage; that at the end of a life of partings, her tears have been wiped away and she is where there are never any more partings or separations ... and she is truly whole. That beautiful God-given mind and smile and best of all, character so beautiful a copy, now perfected, of Jesus Himself, that was fashioned and honed in this place of so many leavings and losses.

As a family we have been so grateful for so many comforting cards, letters, conversations and gracious, generous testimonies to the impact her life had on so many here, and confident expressions of the gospel hope we have for her ... Indeed it is true that she is with the Lord Jesus whom she loved and followed all her life, ... but she would have been severe with me if I implied that our confidence in that was based on how closely she followed Him or how much she loved Him. It is not, and not even with the love-biased, well-intentioned, God-honouring testimony to the quality of her life and service. No. She is home now, because Jesus left His home with the Father to come to earth to find her. She lived, as she lived, always in response to that fact.

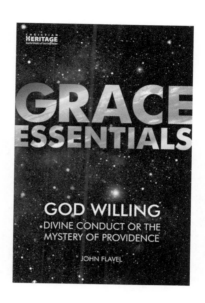

GRACE ESSENTIALS
God Willing
Divine Conduct or the Mystery of Providence
by John Flavel

God works in all parts of our lives, in small things as well as great. These special workings of His providence are not mere accidents. From the day of our birth, to the day of our death, God is working for the good of those who have been called according to His purpose.

In this simplified and abridged form, Flavel addresses how God works providentially in our lives, as well as why and how we should think deeply about these providences. An encouragement to Christians to taste and see the good God has done in our own lives.

ISBN: 978-1-5271-0293-4

I AM

A devotional study of
the attributes of God

BRIAN A. RUSSELL

I AM

A Biblical and Devotional Study
of the Attributes of God
by Brian A. Russell

To have a clearer vision of God should be the Christian's supreme calling, because when we know Him we reflect Him. To love and serve the Creator in righteousness, men and women need something more than an awareness of His existence through general revelation. We also need to know who and what He is, where He can be found, and how He may be approached; He reveals this in His Word. Brian A. Russell here guides us through what the Bible says about the attributes of God.

ISBN: 978-1-5271-0364-1

DAVID & SHIRLEY DONOVAN

COUNTING
THE COST

KIDNAPPED IN THE
NIGER DELTA

COUNTING THE COST
Kidnapped in the Niger Delta
by David & Shirley Donovan

British missionaries David and Shirley Donovan were running a health centre in Nigeria when a pounding on their bedroom door tipped their lives upside down. Threatened at gunpoint, held hostage and ransomed for a billion naira, they tell of the grace that allowed them to witness to their kidnappers in the midst of the chilling and disturbing realisation of what man is capable of.

ISBN: 978-1-5271-0306-1

Christian Focus Publications

Our mission statement —

STAYING FAITHFUL

In dependence upon God we seek to impact the world through literature faithful to His infallible Word, the Bible. Our aim is to ensure that the Lord Jesus Christ is presented as the only hope to obtain forgiveness of sin, live a useful life and look forward to heaven with Him.

Our books are published in four imprints:

CHRISTIAN FOCUS

Popular works including biographies, commentaries, basic doctrine and Christian living.

CHRISTIAN HERITAGE

Books representing some of the best material from the rich heritage of the church.

MENTOR

Books written at a level suitable for Bible College and seminary students, pastors, and other serious readers. The imprint includes commentaries, doctrinal studies, examination of current issues and church history.

CF4•K

Children's books for quality Bible teaching and for all age groups: Sunday school curriculum, puzzle and activity books; personal and family devotional titles, biographies and inspirational stories — because you are never too young to know Jesus!

Christian Focus Publications Ltd,
Geanies House, Fearn, Ross-shire,
IV20 1TW, Scotland, United Kingdom.
www.christianfocus.com
blog.christianfocus.com